Soul to Soul

Fourteen Gatherings for Reflection and Sharing

Christine Robinson and Alicia Hawkins

SKINNER HOUSE BOOKS
BOSTON

Published by Skinner House Books, an imprint of the Unitarian Universalist Association of Congregations, a liberal religious organization with more than 1,000 congregations in the U.S. and Canada, 25 Beacon St., Boston, MA 02108-2800.

www.uua.org/skinner

Printed in the United States

Text design by Suzanne Morgan
Cover art *Circuition 20,* © 2007 Tracey Adams, www.traceyadamsart.com/

print ISBN: 978-1-55896-649-9 / eBook ISBN: 978-1-55896-652-9

6 5 4 3 2 1 / 14 13 12 11

Library of Congress Cataloging-in-Publication Data
Robinson, Christine C.
  Soul to soul : fourteen gatherings for reflection and sharing /
Christine Robinson and Alicia Hawkins.
    p. cm.
  ISBN 978-1-55896-649-9 (pbk. : alk. paper)—ISBN 978-1-55896-652-9
(ebook : alk. paper)
  1. Spiritual life—Unitarian Universalist Association. 2. Church
group work—Unitarian Universalist Association. I. Hawkins, Alicia. II. Title.
  BX9855.R63 2012
  250—dc23
                        2011034792

We gratefully acknowledge the following for permission to reprint copyrighted material:

Carolyn Brown, Shirley Coe, Steve J. Crump, Judy Fjell, Paul Foreman (www.mindmapinspiration.com/riding-the-waves-of-lifes-ups-and-downs),   Tim Haley, Barbara Hamilton-Holway, Maureen Killoran, Gordon B. McKeeman, Peter Morales, Grace Perce.

Excerpt reprinted from *Present Moment, Wonderful Moment: Mindfulness Verses for Daily Living* (1990, 2007) by Thich Nhat Hanh with permission of Parallax Press, Berkeley, California, www.parallax.org.

"On Death," "On Prayer," "The Farewell" from *The Prophet* by Kahlil Gibran, copyright 1923 by Kahlil Gibran and renewed 1951 by Administrators C.T.A. of Kahlil Gibran Estate and Mary G. Gibran. Used by permission of Alfred A. Knopf, a division of Random House, Inc.

Many of our quotes come from historical periods when it was common to use words like "man" and "mankind" semi-generically. We present these quotes as written and intend them to apply to everyone.

Contents

Acknowledgments

This book was written with the help and support of many people, foremost our husbands, William Baker and Charlie Hawkins. Many of the participants in Soul to Soul groups at First Unitarian Church in Albuquerque helped to field test these gatherings. In addition, we are grateful for our partnership in the writing of this book, where Christine Robinson wrote the essays and Alicia Hawkins supplied quotes, poems, and readings and kept on top of the logistics of our project.

Introduction

One evening a woman came to her covenant group with a heavy heart. She had just been diagnosed with breast cancer, her second bout with the disease. From her experience twenty years earlier, she knew how much the treatment would take out of her, and she dreaded what was to come. She told her group that she had spent the past two days bowing out of responsibilities and activities—but that she had decided to stay in her covenant group. "I may need a ride now and then," she said, "but I need your support to get through this."

As the group listened to their distressed member, they became distressed themselves. When she finished her check-in, the leader said simply, "Alicia, we will support you however we can." When the group took its time of silence, Alicia felt waves of support coming toward her from the other group members, and after the meeting, people plied her with offers of rides and meals. "I don't need anything yet," she said, "but if I do, I know where to go."

That day, a little seed was planted in Alicia's heart that ultimately grew into this book. She had always valued the sharing and community that covenant groups provided in her church, and, as a collector of quotations and poetry, she had begun to craft resources for her church's covenant group program. But as she went through her second cancer experience, she realized anew how much the deep support and understanding in her group meant to her and how important it was to her healing. When Alicia started taking on new activities again, her minister, Christine Robinson, suggested they collaborate on a book of resources for covenant groups. Thus they published their first book together, *Heart to Heart*, in 2009, and now follow it up with *Soul to Soul*. In this volume, covenant groups are referred to as Soul to Soul groups.

Christine's experience with these kinds of gatherings came from years of participating in interfaith clergy support and prayer groups. She watched the slow transformation of her church as more and more people were introduced to the concept of deep listening. Parishioners learned to support others without critiquing, posing invasive questions, or making the other usual responses we have been taught in this society. Christine could see boards and committees operating differently. She realized how much pastoral care Soul to Soul groups were providing for the participants and how the groups were helping new members assimilate during a church growth spurt. She, too, wanted to share these blessings with others, both churched and unchurched, because she felt that society can be a better place when people know how to listen deeply to each other and care for one other. There are few places in people's lives where they are invited to share deeply and listen without judgment. The world is hungry for sharing soul to soul.

Deep listening means listening from the heart rather than the mind or ego. It grows out of silence. Deep listening happens when people listen without responding, so they don't have to worry about what to say, what the other person needs to hear, or how to heal the person or solve the problem. In Soul to Soul groups, we listen and breathe, holding the other in our hearts. When someone has shared deeply, our silence tells them we've given them all our attention and that we are holding their story in our hearts. This silence connects us with one another in a way that is deeper than using words or questions.

Heart to Heart opened a way to learn about the power of Soul to Soul groups. Many have seen how these groups enable their members to "grow their souls" and build deeper connections, both within church and neighborhood groups, and between individuals. This book uses the same format with different topics. The structure of a Soul to Soul group allows everyone to talk without being interrupted or questioned.

How to Start a Group

Gather six to eight people who are interested in exploring spiritual or life issues and in deepening their relationships with each other. They may come from within your religious community or other groups or be neighborhood friends. One such group meets after children have been dropped off at school. Another is a conference call between five adult sisters who are scattered across the country. Most commonly, groups form and meet in congregations. You can also use this book by yourself, with journal in hand.

Soul to Soul contains fourteen subjects for gatherings. We recommend that you explore the topics in the order given, as some concepts reoccur. Plan to meet twice a month for about an hour and a half. Each group member will want to have a copy of this book.

Leadership

Once the group becomes accustomed to the gathering format, you may want to take turns leading. Sharing the role of leader can help the group mature, since everyone has an equal stake in running the group. But even if you decide to rotate leadership, there should still be one primary leader who oversees the program and attends to any problems that may come up.

At the end of this book (beginning on page 134), you'll find general notes for leaders and specific notes about each gathering, including what to think about in advance, what to bring, and how to manage tricky issues. It's important to consult these notes before leading a gathering.

Preparation

Each gathering explores a different topic with an essay, quotes, questions, and activities. Participants are encouraged to read the chapter and do the preparatory work before the gathering. Thinking and writing about the topic beforehand fosters more depth. Some group members write their thoughts in a Soul to Soul journal, and others scribble in the margins of their books. One leader gave an inexpensive notebook to each of her group members.

The Gatherings

Each gathering has a consistent structure in order to promote a feeling of safety and encourage interpersonal bonding. Deep listening and sharing are the core of the gathering and will be explained in detail at the first meeting. Each gathering has the following components:

Candle Lighting
On Our Hearts (a brief sharing of general highs and lows in
    members' lives)
Silence
Shared Readings
Sharing (three rounds of sharing by members on the specific
    topic)
Closing Activity
Closing Words
Song (page xiii)
Announcements
Extinguishing the Candle

Before the First Gathering

All participants, including leaders, should read the Introduction of this book and the first gathering, Thick Stories. Read the quotes, essay, and questions, and do the activities in your journal. Dig into the topic. Leaders should also read the Leader's Guide (page 134) and the Leader's Notes for Each Gathering (page 141).

THANK YOU FOR YOUR LOVING HANDS

Music: Judy Fjell ©1982 Lyrics: Lisa Bregger & Judy Fjell©2000

We are excited that you are beginning this journey of deep bonding, community, and spiritual exploration through deep listening and sharing. We hope that you will benefit from considering these topics, deepening friendships, and consistently practicing how to listen. Blessings as you begin!

Thick Stories

CRWO

BEFORE YOU GATHER

Hidden in all stories is the One story. The more we listen, the clearer that story becomes. Our true identity, who we are, why we are here, what sustains us, is in this story. . . . In telling them, we are telling each other the human story.
  —Rachel Naomi Remen

Page by page, chapter by chapter, the story unfolds. Day by day, year by year, your own story unfolds, your life's story.
  —Frederick Buechner

Stories ought not to be just little bits of fantasy that are used to wile away an idle hour; from the beginning of the human race stories have been used—by priests, by bards, by medicine men—as magic instruments of healing, of teaching, as a means of helping people come to terms with the fact that they continually have to face insoluble problems and unbearable realities.
  —Joan Aiken

Stories also reveal the powers that provide orientation in people's lives. When people talk about books or movies that touched them, about people they have loved or wanted to emulate, they speak of that elusive sense of meaning, power, and value that roots their mundane stories in something deeper. This depth dimension of stories is crucial, for without it lives would seem empty, meaningless.

—Carol Christ

Consider This

A few years after Hurricane Katrina, a friend and I (Christine) were taking a cab to the New Orleans airport, and the driver, a native New Orleanian, began to talk about how badly people had behaved during the storm, telling stories from hyped-up news programs he'd watched, all of which we had also heard, some of which had later proved to be false. To get him off that distressing subject, I asked him about his own experience during the storm.

He quickly warmed to the task, telling us that he had, indeed, lost everything in the flooding, but that he had held property insurance with a good insurance company. Further, he had been employed as a manager at Wal-Mart, and when he reported to work in Baton Rouge (to which he had been evacuated), they promptly paid him and set him the task of returning to New Orleans as soon as possible, armed with the authority to give out $2,000 checks to every employee of his old store that he could find. He remembered with pleasure the experience of being trusted in that extraordinary way and of being able to give such generous help to his coworkers. Our ride to the airport went all too quickly as we listened, fascinated and moved by his wonderful story. That was one cab ride that ended a lot better than it started. All I had done, really, was redirect the cabbie away from oft-repeated gossip about events neither of us had experienced, and toward his own experiences of those profound weeks. As often happens when people tell their personal stories, I didn't have to prod or interpret. I hardly said a word between my question and my thank-you as we paid him at the airport, and this wonderful story came pouring out, thick as molasses. Whenever the subject of Hurricane Katrina comes up, I remember it still.

We attempt to do two things in Soul to Soul groups. We give ourselves permission to tell thick stories, and we practice thick listening. While nearly everybody can tell a thick story when they talk about themselves, thick listening is a new skill which we have to practice.

When we speak from our hearts and talk about ourselves—saying what has happened to us, how we believe and feel and think—we find not only that we have gained from hearing ourselves, but that our stories have been interesting to others in the group. Telling a thick story feels risky, but once we decide to take the risk, it is easy to do well. Everybody can do a good job telling their own story. Many find that knowing there will be no arguments, no probing questions, and no "helpful comments" to which they will have to respond gives them the courage to share things that they would otherwise keep to themselves. It is not at all uncommon in a Soul to Soul group to hear, after a particularly wonderful story, "I have never talked about that before."

It *is* a bit risky to talk personally in a group, especially when we don't know the other people, and that is one reason we so often resort to chitchat or tell stories about other people. No doubt the cabbie started with his thin story of other people's misdeeds during Katrina because he didn't know us, his riders. He didn't know our politics, our attitudes about race, our feeling about his home town. It was safe to tell a story everybody had already heard. Nor was he a bragging sort of man. He had to be invited to tell his thick story about what happened to him during Katrina. He had to feel like we were really interested in what he had to say. He had to feel safe. And that means we had to listen as thickly as he was speaking.

We could have blown it at any moment. We could have launched into our own experiences during storms. We could have made a remark that sounded condescending. We could have argued about the politics of Walmart. We sidestepped all of these possibilities because we invited him to talk and then we just listened, encouraging him mostly with meaningless sounds that showed him we were on the same emotional wavelength. That's all we did. It may not sound like much, but it is crucial. Most people find it difficult to just listen.

Our culture teaches us thin listening skills. We quickly pick up that we should show we've been paying attention by asking pointed questions or giving wise advice. Neither strategy, it turns out, feels very good to the person who just spoke. Often our advice is ill-fitting, or the person to whom it is addressed—who is, after all, different from us—is not ready to hear it. Almost all of us are more likely to follow up on our own good ideas than someone else's! And even the most well-meant and gently spoken questions can feel like criticism. As for launching into our own story that we were reminded of, well, that's a fine ploy for conversation, but when our intention is to simply listen, we need to restrain ourselves. The healing power of this kind of listening is attested to by Parker Palmer in *A Hidden Wholeness*:

> When you speak to me about your deepest questions, you do not want to be fixed or saved: you want to be seen and heard, to have your truth acknowledged and honored. If your problem is soul-deep, your soul alone knows what you need to do about it, and my presumptuous advice will only drive your soul back into the woods. So the best service I can render when you speak to me about such a struggle is to hold you faithfully in a space where you can listen to your inner teacher. Most of us, so carefully schooled in our need to be actively helpful to people, are very surprised to discover the healing power of this kind of listening.

Even therapists and ministers in training commonly imagine that they have to "do something" to be helpful to the person who is speaking to them and are surprised to hear that they were very helpful even though they couldn't think of a thing to say! "But all I did was listen!" they protest, and their teachers say knowingly, "Precisely!" So while we might say, "hmm!" or "wow!" or make other encouraging noises at appropriate points, we will mostly remain silent, not only outwardly, by not talking much, but inwardly, by attending to what is being said. Since we don't have to probe or give advice, we don't have to be thinking ahead to what we will say. We can simply listen and offer the speaker the gift of silence. Rachel Naomi Remen says,

> Perhaps the most important thing we bring to another person is the silence in us. Not the sort of silence that is filled with unspoken criticism or hard withdrawal. The sort of silence that is a place of refuge, of rest, of acceptance of someone as they are. We are all hungry for this other silence. It is hard to find. In its presence we can remember something beyond the moment, a strength on which to build a life. Silence is a place of great power and healing.

Our cabbie's story ended when we arrived at the airport and had to part company. We thanked him for sharing, paid him, and went inside. But after a story is told in a Soul to Soul group, it is less clear how to end the interaction. People ask what they can do after someone has shared—particularly early on in the group's life. Silence can feel awkward and even uncaring at first. It takes some experience in speaking and listening for people to understand how powerful and appreciative simple silence can be, and how knowing that there will be no questions, comments, or side conversations bolsters the sharing. So, at first, some groups adopt a small ritual of response. Sometimes the leader simply says thank you. In some groups everyone smiles at the speaker, and some use hands in prayer-mode with a little bow. Even after these responses, we suggest that there be some silence, perhaps half a minute or so, before the next person starts sharing. This silence gives space for everyone to finish listening and to appreciate having been allowed into the recesses of the speaker's life. The sense of intimacy is rich and sacred. When the heart is speaking and the heart is listening, silence becomes fulfilling. After some practice at this, the early awkwardness is gone and the silence becomes as rich as a river of love flowing to and from the listener. That's the magic of Soul to Soul groups.

Activity

To help people get to know each other, we ask you to bring something to this first gathering that symbolizes for you one of the deep and meaningful parts of your life. We hope that this will help you to take a little more risk in sharing than you might usually do in a new group. It is our hope and prayer that you will find that sharing of yourself, and helping others share of themselves, will be a source of great joy and blessing.

One participant in a group like this brought her grandmother's quilt and talked about connections to women through the generations. Another brought her journal and spoke of her own inner journey. Someone brought his garden spade and shared his deep love of working the earth. A child's photograph helped one person speak about the meaning of parenthood. As you think about what is most deeply meaningful to you, no doubt you will also find something to symbolize it!

Questions to Ponder

1. What is your favorite story about yourself? What is a favorite story about you as a child?

2. What is a favorite story about you and your parents or grandparents?

3. What is one thing you hope the group learns about you in these next few months?

4. Write a story or memory that speaks about who you really are.

Think about the item you will bring to the gathering and how you will share it. What does this item tell about you?

~

GATHERING

Welcome and Explanations   10 minutes

Candle Lighting

East: Brother Fire, we invoke warmth. May our hearts be open to each other.

South: Father Air, we invoke inspiration. May our words be wise and kind.

West: Sister Water, we invoke the flow of life. May we have courage.

North: Mother Earth, we invoke groundedness. May we all be here in spirit as well as in body.

Leader: Spirit within, we invoke depth. May we remember all we value.

Covenant and Ground Rules

I commit myself:

- to come to meetings when I possibly can, knowing that my presence is important to the group;
- to let the leader know if I will be absent or need to quit;
- to share with the leader the responsibility for good group process by watching how much time I take to speak and noticing what is going on for others;
- to do the reading and thinking about the topic ahead of time;
- to not gossip about what is shared in the group, and tell only my own story to others;
- to honor the safety of the group by listening to what others share with an open heart;

- to refrain from cross-talk, judging, or giving advice;
- and to share as deeply as I can when it is my turn.

Silence   3 minutes

Shared Readings

To laugh is to risk appearing the fool.
To weep is to risk appearing sentimental.
To reach out for another is to risk exposing our true self.
To place our ideas—our dreams—before the crowd is to risk loss.
To love is to risk not being loved in return.
To hope is to risk despair.
To try is to risk failure.
To live is to risk dying.
   —Anonymous

The truth of it is that if you really listen to another person, whether on the surface he is talking about the weather or predicting the outcome of the World Series or even preaching a sermon, if you really listen, you begin to realize that what he is really talking about is himself. He is saying, "Love me," or maybe "Hate me" or "Pity me," but always he is saying one way or another, "Listen to me. Know me."
   —Frederick Buechner

The greatest gift we bring to the listening process is ourselves. And the most important thing to do in order to listen well is to keep ourselves out of the way. Here we have a fundamental paradox in listening.
   —Emma J. Justes

There are only two or three human stories, and they go on repeating themselves as fiercely as if they had never happened before.
   —Willa Cather

Sharing   60 minutes

Closing Activity

Closing Words

Listening is the oldest and perhaps most powerful tool of healing. It is often through the quality of our listening and the wisdom of our words that we are able to effect the most profound changes in the people around us.
—Rachel Naomi Remen

Song

Announcements

Extinguishing the Candle

East: Brother Fire, we thank you for warming our hearts.
South: Father Air, we thank you for inspiring us here.
West: Sister Water, we thank you for the courage to be present
          to the flow of life.
North: Mother Earth, we thank you for grounding us here.
Leader: Spirit within, we take you with us to cherish until we
          meet again.

Compassion

∾

BEFORE YOU GATHER

A deep distress hath humanized my soul.
—William Wordsworth

Do not believe that he who seeks to comfort you lives untroubled among the simple and quiet words that sometimes do you good. His life has much difficulty and sadness and remains far behind yours. Were it otherwise he would never have been able to find those words.
—Rainer Maria Rilke

Compassion is the sometimes fatal capacity for feeling what it's like to live inside somebody else's skin. It is the knowledge that there can never really be any peace and joy for me until there is peace and joy finally for you too.
—Frederick Buechner

The whole idea of compassion is based on a keen awareness of the interdependence of all these living beings, which are all part of one another, and all involved in one another.
—Thomas Merton

The only reason that we don't open our hearts and minds to other people is that they trigger confusion in us that we don't feel brave enough or sane enough to deal with. To the degree that we look clearly and compassionately at ourselves, we feel confident and fearless about looking into someone else's eyes.

—Pema Chödrön

Consider This

Compassion is feeling with another person who is in pain (com = with, passion = suffering). In compassion, we sacrifice our comfort to be helpful to a hurting person. The nuances of this word place it between pity, which is feeling but distancing, as in "those people over there, how they suffer," and empathy, a word which has connotations of "feeling with," but in an enmeshed, unboundaried way. Neither pity nor empathy are useful to a suffering person. Only compassion is close enough to be helpful, but distant enough to be effective. Compassion, in other words, is feeling with others, but with appropriate boundaries.

Think of it this way. In a roadside accident, most people will rubberneck and drive on, thinking, "Those poor people. They must have been drinking. That will never happen to me." This is, of course, useless to the victims, and if they heard it, it would be painful to them. It's just too much distance. A few people will stop and try to help, but they will so empathize with the pain of the victims that they will panic. Human as this is, it is also useless to sufferers. Only the person who is both close enough to help and emotionally distanced enough to stay calm and focused on the victim can actually do any good.

Research shows that empathy really does hurt. Let's say we come across someone who has just broken an ankle; the parts of our brain that light up on an MRI scan are the same as if we had broken our own ankle. When we witness a severe trauma, unless we have learned to put some boundaries between ourselves and others, our bodies might even begin to go into shock. Empathy is actually not a good thing. Disaster scenes require appropriate boundaries, but so do less fraught helping situations. If someone begins to tell me about their grief over their grandmother, and I over-identify with their grief (probably because I have not processed some grief of my own), I will not be able to be helpful. I will interrupt, give advice based on my own experience, and become too anxious to be a good listener, or I will become mute and withdraw into my own pain. Compassion takes energy, self discipline, and significant sacrifice.

At the other extreme of reacting to another's suffering is pity: noticing, but with no identification at all. We react as if our situation is so different from the sufferer's that we could never imagine being in the same place. "I don't live in a neighborhood like that," we comfort ourselves after hearing about a brutal street crime. "Did he smoke?" we ask when we are told of someone's lung cancer. This kind of distancing will almost certainly go on in our minds; it is a psychological defense, and the skillful person will notice it and let it pass. Often, however, our anxieties are so great that we trouble the person in pain with our theories, our questions, and the walls we have erected between us in our minds, and we hurt them further. This defense mechanism is called "blaming the victim," and we see individuals, groups, and even nations indulging in it.

Compassion is the middle ground of "feeling with." A compassionate person can be with a sufferer because she knows that suffering is part of the human condition, including her own. She also knows that she is not this sufferer, so she has the energy to be a calm or helpful presence.

The development of non-anxious compassion is a major goal of Buddhist teachings and practices. Sitting quietly and watching our mind's defenses and distractions while keeping a sense of open-heartedness for the world is a skill that one can develop. Studies show that even a modest amount of this kind of practice changes how we think about others and increases our willingness to be helpful. Other religious traditions suggest praying for others, which requires similar skills and mindset.

Among the many benefits of developing compassion is that the same skills we use to tolerate and be helpful in others' suffering can help us be compassionate to ourselves, if we will only use them. It seems that many compassionate people do not think to do this. Research shows that many people who find it easy to be kind to others, forgive their shortcomings, and accept them in spite of their flaws are very hard on themselves!

That very lack of self-compassion puts us in some danger of depression and other emotional ills, and these, of course, make it hard, if not impossible, to care about others.

Once again, there is wisdom about balancing compassion and self-compassion in the world's religions. Buddhist teacher Pema Chodron points out that our compassion should go to whomever in our life is most in need of it, and often that will be ourselves. "Love thy neighbor as thyself," as Jesus said, is not just an injunction to be concerned with others; it requires appropriate self-love as well. And psychologists tell us that one emotion is simply impossible without the other. Those who would love others must also love themselves. They tell us this on airplanes all the time: If you are caring for a child and the masks fall from the ceiling, put your own mask on first, and then help your child. If you don't, you'll faint and be useless.

Researchers at Wake Forest University found that people who find it difficult to be kind to themselves often believe that doing so would lower their standards or cause them to lose self-control, but the opposite seems true: The less we beat up on ourselves, the more self-control we experience. In a carefully designed study, researchers determined that subjects who thought they had been recruited as taste-testers of candy ate less, not more, when they were encouraged to take it easy on themselves for eating extra sweets. Excused from the reflexive need to feel badly about yielding to temptation, they didn't need to soothe themselves with sweets. (This demonstrates the problem of making a willful assault on our addictions. We fail in self-control, give ourselves a scolding, feel bad, and are all the more prey to the very addiction we are trying to overcome!)

Self-compassion is actually a better strategy for self-control, just as compassion encourages others to have self-control.

Researcher Kristin Neff says that self-compassion consists of three things: kindness to one's self, the ability to moderate our negative emotions, and the understanding that "people (including us) are like that." She also notes that self-compassion is not self-indulgence, which is giving in to desires or moods with no regard to overall health. Rather, self-compassion acts for the long-term well-being of the self. It's also not self-pity, which is an isolated immersion in one's problems. People who are experiencing self-pity think that their suffering is unique, whereas self-compassionate people know that almost anything that afflicts them has happened to many other people.

Ironically, the greatest enemy of self-compassion is pride. Excessively prideful people see themselves as standing above the crowd, and they usually hold themselves to very high standards. Because those are hard to maintain and a pinnacle is a lonely place to be, they become emotionally brittle and punish themselves (and often those around them) when they don't measure up. For them, the first step toward self-compassion *and* compassion is to come down off that pinnacle, give up some of that self-imposed distance, and join humanity.

And so we circle back to boundaries and come at last to compassion burn-out, which is, simply, the need to withdraw from suffering long enough to restore battered boundaries or return from the dispassionate distance our caring has required of us. The EMT who must work skillfully with people in terrible pain has to reopen her heart before she goes home to her children with their everyday hurts. The disaster helper who finds that he is beginning to weep uncontrollably with clients needs to take some time for healing and rebuild the appropriate emotional walls which will allow him to listen without over-empathizing. These tasks are different from simple rest (which they no doubt also need). They are a rebuilding of the self after the sacrifices of compassion. And when they are done well, most of us discover that our open hearts are bottomless;

that a love that supports us and those we care for wells up unbidden and gives us strengths we never knew we had.

Activities

1. Moving toward compassion is an action of the heart rather than the mind. The Eastern Orthodox Church practices this heart connection with The Prayer of the Heart, a practice from early Christianity of praying from a prayer word and breath. It is sometimes called the Jesus Prayer or the Prayer of Unceasing. Pick a word or phrase which springs from the heart concerning compassion, such as, "May I grow in compassion" or "Open my heart" or "Mercy and kindness." This phrase may be synchronized with part of the phrase on the in-breath and the rest of the phrase on the out-breath, or with the whole phrase being thought or said on the out-breath. Repeat this over and over. If thoughts distract you, let them go and come back to the breath phrase spoken from the heart.

2. Some find that a prayer rope is helpful in focusing while doing the Prayer of the Heart. Tie from ten to twenty knots in a piece of yarn or twine. Move your fingers from one knot to another, saying the prayer to yourself and breathing at each knot. The prayer rope can be carried in your pocket, and without being seen, you can move your hand from knot to knot, saying the phrase.

3. Think of a time in the past few weeks that you have given or received compassion. Write down the circumstances, the way you felt, who was there, the words that were said. How did you feel when you came away from the experience? Take a snapshot in your mind. Now, write about this experience. Here's one such snapshot:

The Child

She comes to me weeping.
My arms enfold her,
Gently we rock
In silence deeper than words.
The trembling stills,
Breathing becomes slow and even.
She kisses me, murmurs "thanks,"
And climbs back within me.
We move out to greet the day.
  —Alicia Hawkins

Questions to Ponder

1. What memory of compassion stands out for you? Did you give it or receive it? How has it affected your life today?

2. What does it mean to have compassion for yourself? How have you noticed compassion and self-compassion interacting?

3. When faced with the suffering of the whole world, how do you cope with the limits of your compassion?

4. Who is easy for you to feel compassion for? Who is difficult to extend compassion to? Do you know why?

5. What would a discipline of compassion look like in your life? What would it consist of?

6. How have your life experiences affected your ability to be compassionate?

Think about an experience you've had in the past few weeks in giving, receiving, or observing compassion that you are willing to share with the group.

❧

GATHERING

Candle Lighting

East: Brother Fire, we invoke warmth. May our hearts be open to each other.

South: Father Air, we invoke inspiration. May our words be wise and kind.

West: Sister Water, we invoke the flow of life. May we have courage.

North: Mother Earth, we invoke groundedness. May we all be here in spirit as well as in body.

Leader: Spirit within, we invoke depth. May we remember all we value.

On Our Hearts   10 minutes

Silence   3 minutes

Shared Readings

You may call God love, you may call God goodness. But the best name for God is compassion.
    —Meister Eckhart

One kind word can warm three winter months.
　　—Japanese proverb

Kindness is the shadow of God in man.
　　—Kahlil Gibran

We need to increase the scope of our compassion until it embraces all living beings without exception, just as a loving mother feels compassion for all her children regardless of whether they are behaving well or badly.
　　—Geshe Kelsang Gyatso

Waking up this morning, I smile.
Twenty-four brand new hours are before me.
I vow to live fully in each moment
and to look at all beings with eyes of compassion.
　　—Thich Nhat Hanh

Sharing　　60 minutes

Closing Activity

Closing Words

If you want others to be happy, practice compassion; and if you want yourself to be happy, practice compassion.
　　—Dalai Lama

Song

Announcements

Extinguishing the Candle

East: Brother Fire, we thank you for warming our hearts.

South: Father Air, we thank you for inspiring us here.

West: Sister Water, we thank you for the courage to be present to the flow of life.

North: Mother Earth, we thank you for grounding us here.

Leader: Spirit within, we take you with us to cherish until we meet again.

Boundaries

❧

BEFORE YOU GATHER

And this is one of the major questions of our lives: how we keep boundaries, what permission we have to cross boundaries, and how we do so.
—A.B. Yehoshua

The great task is to claim yourself for yourself, so that you can contain your needs within the boundaries of your self and hold them in the presence of those you love. True mutuality in love requires people who possess themselves and who can give to each other while holding on to their own identities. So, in order both to give more effectively and to be more self-contained with your needs, you must learn to set boundaries to your love.
—Henri Nouwen

True intimacy is possible only between two whole, distinct people who both have good boundaries. Enmeshment feels like intimacy but it's not. How can you be intimate with someone who blends into you? Intimacy grows as you become known by the other and as you know the other. If the other person's individuality shifts and fades, how can you know this person? If your sense of yourself is wobbly, how can you be known?
—Anne Katherine

Consider This

Consider the lowly cell, one part of many interconnecting systems in, say, the skin of your finger. That cell has a center, the nucleus with its DNA instructions as to what the cell is supposed to do, and a boundary, the cell wall. A living, healthy cell is crystal clear about its instructions, and if something happens to change those instructions, problems such as cancers arise. In a living, healthy cell, the boundary is permeable: The appropriate things can get in and out. Nourishment has to get in through the cell wall, for instance, and waste has to get out. Without this give and take with the systems it is connected to, the cell quickly dies. But it also quickly dies if its wall is breached beyond repair or becomes too permeable. Then the cell's contents float out and it can't function as an entity at all. Every cell has to have its integrity, its job within the system, and an appropriate boundary.

An individual person also has a physical boundary, the skin, and if that skin becomes too broken or too unyielding, the person's health takes a dramatic turn for the worse. However, when we speak of a person's boundaries, we are usually talking not about our physical selves but our social selves, and the importance of functioning well in the social systems of which we are a part. We humans are both individual selves and beings who function in systems. We need, like a cell and like a body, to know who we are, what we are supposed to be doing, and how we are feeling. We need an appropriate boundary, one that both lets things in—knowledge, for instance, and love, and signals from others around us—and lets things out, allowing us to communicate with others, work with them, and care for them. To have appropriate boundaries means that we respect ourselves, our tasks, and our feelings, and we are in touch with the systems around us. These two things work together in most people to produce a strong sense of respect for the people around us, their tasks, thoughts, and feelings. We don't confuse ourselves with others, and we can stay in relationships without losing ourselves.

We've probably all known someone whose boundaries are way too broad and make us feel encroached on. They might stand too close to us, feel hurt if we don't share their tastes, or do way too much for us. They might ask questions which are too personal, violate our privacy, share our stories too broadly, or expect personal or even sexual favors without regard to our needs and desires. Those are all cases of boundaries that are way too open and loose.

On the other hand, we've probably all known people whose boundaries are too rigid. They have a hard time taking in new information or getting to know new people. They have difficulty with give-and-take. If they don't get their way, even in minor things, they feel threatened to the core of their being. They just don't get along. They have a hard time being affectionate, even with their spouses and children.

Appropriate boundaries change as situations change. A caregiver will grab the back of a toddler's pants to stop him from running off. But the caregiver of a disabled or sick adult will be much more respectful when guiding their footsteps, for adults have strong boundaries about physical contact.

Growing children will protest, "I can do it!" when they are given too much help, and good parents, delighted to see their growing independence and skill, will let them do things on their own—even though it will take much more time!

Negotiating changes in appropriate boundaries is one of the greatest challenges of parenting and growing up. Our culture has many cautionary stories about parents whose boundaries overlap their children's inappropriately. We talk of "stage moms," who seem to be living their own unrealized dreams through their children, or "helicopter parents," who drop in to rescue their college students at the first woeful phone call home. Advice columnists regularly counsel young adults to (gently) tell well-meaning parents to let them and their spouses have privacy and boundaries. The part of the wedding service where parents acknowledge that their children are moving on to a new phase of life is one of the most important parts of a wedding. Parents have needed help establishing good boundaries with their children since time immemorial.

Then, later in life, boundaries change again as parents age, needing more and more help. Grown children sometimes need to take over a parent's care, finances, and decisions, which often feels like an uncomfortable softening of boundaries.

To some extent, boundaries are social constructs. How close we stand to each other, whether friends kiss on the lips, how personal a conversation should be, and who are considered appropriate sex partners are different in each culture. Yet, even though we know that these are just social constructs, we become very uncomfortable when they are violated. Unless we have agreed with someone that we do not need to honor these conventions, we should be on our guard around people who don't honor small boundaries until we are sure they will honor important ones.

When our boundaries are crossed, we don't just notice the error, we feel it. A person who stands too close or asks questions that are too personal irritates us. If the boundary crossing is severe enough, such as rape, we feel violated to the core of our being. And on the other hand, if our boundaries harden too much, we become isolated, lonely, and out of touch.

In this, as in so many important parts of our lives, we have to strike a balance between boundaries that are too soft and those that are too hard. In relationships, we need to both have a strong sense of who we are and stay in touch with those around us. Most of us do one or the other more naturally, and when we are stressed, we tend to overdo our natural inclination. It's not at all uncommon for a person who is normally easy to be around to become hyper in a family emergency, bustling around making plans for other people or trying to get them to eat when they are not hungry. The crisis brings out their need to be a little too enmeshed with others. On the other hand, we've all known people who respond to a crisis by withdrawing or becoming prickly; their boundaries become too rigid.

As we think about this balance, we can remember the helpful motto, "Be a self and stay in touch." Healthy, ongoing relationships have to have both strong and loose boundaries. If there's too much "stay in touch," we become enmeshed. If we can only think about ourselves and what we want and need, we become isolated. On the other hand, if we are unclear about what we want and need, it will be hard, not only for us but also for those around us, to function well. Consider a couple trying to decide what to do next weekend. One person proposes several alternatives, expecting to negotiate needs. This is an appropriate way for two selves to get their needs met. The second person says she doesn't really care what they do. This might seem generous, but actually, it throws a monkey wrench into the works. The first person now has to either dictate what the couple will do or try to guess what the other person wants and hope it works out. Whatever the decision, resentment is the likely result. This is not a healthy pattern. It takes two strong selves, who know what they want *and* who plan to do the work of staying in touch (negotiating differing wants, in this case), to make a strong relationship that has good boundaries.

Groups of people also have boundaries that help the group function. In Soul to Soul groups, for instance, it is clear who is in the group. People don't bring their spouses or houseguests; that would be a violation of the group's boundaries and make people uncomfortable. It is clear what the rules of confidentiality are and how long the group will last. These boundaries help people be comfortable in the group.

Robert Frost wrote, "Good fences make good neighbors." This wisdom describes the importance of good boundaries in human relationships and the effectiveness of both having a strong self and staying in touch with the strong selves of those around us.

Activities

1. We learn powerful lessons about appropriate boundaries by being part of a family. Think back to your family as you were growing up. Who was distant, and who was close? Did you ever feel that you were enmeshed with someone else? Using the

models below to give you some ideas, draw your own family diagram.

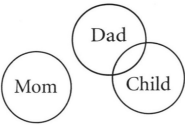

Parents are estranged from each other, Dad is probably too involved with the child, and Mom is too distant.

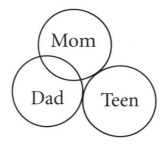

Mom and Dad have a solid relationship. The teen knows they are there for him but is establishing his own life.

Helping aging parents requires a softening of boundaries.

2. On the list of boundary violations below, put a checkmark by the ones that really irritate or offend you, a small circle by those that don't bother you at all, and a question mark by the ones which you don't understand how they might be considered boundary violations.

Someone standing too close to you

Someone interrupting you when you are speaking

Someone finishing your sentences

Helping professionals becoming romantically involved with people they are helping

Adults insisting on hugging and kissing children who they don't know well

Someone insisting on helping you when you've indicated you don't need help

Someone telling a story about you to others (not necessarily a secret, just a story)

Someone touching a pregnant woman's belly

Someone slapping your back

Someone (with good intentions) doing part of your work for you

Someone commenting about your weight, health, age, ethnicity, hair color, salary, or some other aspect of your life that you consider private

Someone insisting on petting your dog

A friend walking into your house without knocking

A family member opening the bathroom door while you are bathing

Now, think about whether you ever do some of these things. If so, are you sure it's okay? Can you check this out with the people involved? ("You know, Joe, I realize that I ask you about your weight loss often. Is that okay with you? I mean to be encouraging, but I just want to make sure. . . .")

Questions to Ponder

1. Have there been times in your life when you felt too involved in another person's life, or they in yours? What happened? How did things change? How do you feel about that experience?

2. When people are hurt, they often overreact to protect themselves and create overly rigid boundaries, thinking, "No one can hurt me now!" When and with whom have you created a rigid boundary to hide behind?

3. Think about boundaries in your family that are shifting now or have changed over the years. Describe a time when you consciously decided to soften, firm up, or alter your boundaries.

4. If you have a tendency to be a people-pleaser (have weak boundaries), list a couple of ways you might change this tendency. Think of someone who bullies you into accepting his/her ideas. What are some different ways to deal with this person?

Think about a time when you let down your boundaries in order to please people or about ways in which boundaries have changed in your family. Decide what you are willing to share with the group.

∾

GATHERING

Candle Lighting

East: Brother Fire, we invoke warmth. May our hearts be open to each other.

South: Father Air, we invoke inspiration. May our words be wise and kind.

West: Sister Water, we invoke the flow of life. May we have courage.

North: Mother Earth, we invoke groundedness. May we all be here in spirit as well as in body.

Leader: Spirit within, we invoke depth. May we remember all we value.

On Our Hearts   10 minutes

Silence   3 minutes

Shared Readings

Trees need their protective bark to enable the delicate process of growth and renewal to unfold without threat. Likewise, we must have our boundaries and defenses so that the more vulnerable parts of ourselves can safely heal and unfold. But our growth also depends upon our ability to soften, loosen, and discard boundaries and defenses that we no longer need. It is often the case in life that structures we put in place to help us grow eventually become constricting.
   —Madisyn Taylor

Compassion means to suffer with, but it doesn't mean to get lost in the suffering, so that it becomes exclusively one's own. I tend to do this, to replace the person for whom I am feeling compassion with myself.
   —Madeleine L'Engle

Good boundaries enable us to define ourselves. They enhance our physical and emotional health and promote recovery. Good boundaries yield healthy relationships.
   —Anne Katherine

Sharing   60 minutes

Closing Activity

Closing Words

Healthy boundaries are both firm and flexible—they bend with the blowing wind and stand sturdy through the storms of life.
    —Martha Baldwin Beveridge

Song

Announcements

Extinguishing the Candle

East: Brother Fire, we thank you for warming our hearts.

South: Father Air, we thank you for inspiring us here.

West: Sister Water, we thank you for the courage to be present to the flow of life.

North: Mother Earth, we thank you for grounding us here.

Leader: Spirit within, we take you with us to cherish until we meet again.

Trust

∾

BEFORE YOU GATHER

Trust building is hard to do. It requires an investment of the heart.
—Parker Palmer

No one is born knowing how to trust. Life gives us many teachers, some caring and others cruel. Few people receive a solid base of trust as children. Even fewer are taught how to trust themselves.
—Cynthia L. Wall

And the day came when the risk to remain tight in a bud was more painful than the risk it took to blossom.
—attributed to Anaïs Nin

Unwavering trust is a rare and precious thing because it often demands a degree of courage that borders on the heroic.
—Brennan Manning

Trust is the glue of life. It's the most essential ingredient in effective communication. It's the foundational principle that holds all relationships . . . together.
—Stephen R. Covey

We're never so vulnerable than when we trust someone—but paradoxically, if we cannot trust, neither can we find love or joy.

—Walter Anderson

Consider This

The baby wakes to strangeness. Still new to life, already she has learned a vital lesson: "Cry brings comfort." She begins to wail. Nearby, a loving caregiver stops what he is doing and comes. His very presence is comfort, and the baby relaxes. He feeds, burps, changes, plays. All these things are important, even lifesaving, for the baby. But just as important is what the baby has learned: "I can trust the world. I know what to expect. I will be cared for. It's okay."

The word *trust* comes from the German *trost*, which means solace or comfort. It's got a much bigger meaning in English, but it starts with learning that we can count on care and comfort when we are helpless babies. On that foundation of basic trust, psychologists say, each of us builds all that is our lives. Most babies are born with a high default trust setting; they will relax into the arms of anybody who cares for them. A baby who feels hunger, cries, and is fed begins to know what hunger feels like, begins to predict the future, begins to trust her body as well as those around her and the world in general. While some of us have a more secure foundation than others, all of us received enough care to survive, and therefore even those who experienced neglect in their early years still have significant stores of trust.

Perhaps it is because trust is so primal that we Americans rate this quality as the most important aspect of a relationship. Whether it's our lover or our doctor, more than anything else we want to trust that person so we can continue to believe, "I can trust the world. I know what to expect. I will be cared for. It's okay." Of course, as we get older, we begin to expect more abstract results of our trust: We trust someone who tells us the truth, who keeps promises, whose actions are predictable. We're often disappointed.

Once out of infancy, we embark on a life of adventure in trusting. We continue to amass experiences that help us put our trust in what is actually trustworthy. We learn to trust, not in general, but also in particular: Mother will come. Daddy will do what he promised. My friend will tell me the truth even when it is hard. God will provide, in the end. And, on the other hand: I can't trust this babysitter to be kind to me. I can't trust the church to tell me the whole truth. I can't trust this lover, who has betrayed me twice now. Because individuals and institutions are fallible and God unfathomable, we will regularly experience what seem to us to be breaches of trust. From the appointment not kept to the confidence betrayed to the affair revealed, we wail, "But I thought I could *trust* you!" Not only does the relationship seem fragile, our whole world seems to teeter, just a little, when we feel betrayed. And it never teeters as much as when we realize that we should not have been so trusting, which is to say, that we can't completely trust ourselves and our own perceptions.

Over our lives, we build on our foundation of basic trust with specific experiences of trust, gullibility, cynicism, and reconciliation after breaches of trust. Our experiences give us a sort of default trust setting, an attitude with which we face the world. Our default setting not only shapes our own feelings and behavior, it also shapes the way others behave toward us. It might seem that a cynical attitude is safest, but since people who sense that they are not trusted often withdraw from a relationship and sometimes even act in untrustworthy ways, it is actually a terrible risk. And while the happy-go-lucky, "trust the universe" stance might seem like an advanced spiritual practice, in actuality, it can invite exploitation.

Ironically, gullibility—or unwarranted trust—is usually caused by lack of trust in oneself and one's own intuition, judgment, and ability to affect the world. If I don't trust myself and my own perceptions, those around me will have an undue influence on me. People who have survived long periods of hard knocks—times when they really were out of control and associating with people who were stressed (and therefore less trustworthy)—often emerge from those experiences with a lack of trust in themselves.

Because our default trust setting is so crucial to our success in life and relationships, it's important to notice and tend to it as best we can. If our default setting is too skeptical, we need to understand where our lack of trust came from, work at taking the risks of trust, and make sure that we celebrate the trusting relationships we have. We need to understand our tendency to leap to the conclusion that we have been betrayed whenever something disappointing happens to us, rather than to find out what really happened—often a miscommunication or extenuating circumstances which are perfectly understandable. On the other hand, if we tend to trust too much, we also need to ask why, and take the risk of noticing and trusting our inner wisdom and body's messages. With these kinds of awareness, we can face the world with good balance.

Developing trust when our inclination is to be skeptical is a process—whether that trust is in life, a person, or ourselves. Redeveloping trust after betrayal also takes time and effort. That process is best undertaken through awareness, baby steps, and accountability.

Let's say that my thirteen-year-old daughter has, after a childhood of learning to tell the truth and keep promises, misstepped badly, and I feel betrayed. How do I redevelop my trust in her? First, I must become aware of what has really happened—both to her, to cause this problem, and within myself. That takes a frank conversation, always best done after feelings have had a chance to fade a bit. I must ask myself if I had a part in this incident. If so, I need to own up to that, saying something like, "Honey, I see that I have been thinking of you as a younger child, and I hear you say that your frustration with that helped cause this problem. You're thirteen, a teen, and I have to get used to that. It would have been better if we'd had this conversation before this incident happened. Now I have to regain my trust in you."

I have to ask myself, "Are my feelings now caused just by this incident, or are they hooking into other feelings? What do I know about adolescents that illuminates this incident? What do I remember about my adolescence that might help me with this situation?" My awareness can come from some time spent with my journal, from talking to my partner or other parents, and even, if I find myself distressed enough, in therapy. But without awareness of what is really going on, any redevelopment of trust will be shallow.

Second, I will make some small agreements with my daughter to allow her to re-establish her trustworthiness. We'll create some accountability: She will show me her homework instead of just asserting that it is done. She will call when she gets to her friend's house and put her friend's mother on the line so I am sure of her whereabouts, just for a while. Naturally, being thirteen, she will complain that I should just trust her. And that will give me the opportunity to teach her that we all earn trust, and when we breach trust, this is how we re-earn it.

Parents know that teaching trustworthiness is part of our job, and we know that children will misstep as they grow in this area. That makes it easier to back up and apply awareness, baby steps, and accountability. It's harder for us when an adult breaches our trust; we sense that this is a much more serious issue. We are more likely to feel hurt. However, the steps of reconciliation are the same.

When we realize that we have been too trusting or have somehow breached our own trust in ourselves, the process is similar: We have to become aware of all aspects of the problem, find some baby steps to risk reconciliation, and develop strategies of accountability to make that risk feel comfortable.

All this is hard work, but it is important. It is in our best interest to maintain our default trust setting solidly between "gullible" and "cynical" to preserve both our spiritual health and the good relationships on which our happiness rests.

Activities

1. Write a short reflection about trust in your life: how you feel when you trust another, how trust affects relationships with others, how you have rebuilt broken trust, etc.

2. Think back over the years into your childhood, teen years, young adult years, middle age. What are some highs and lows in your adventures with trust? Make a timeline with notations about these times. Who have been your teachers of trust, "some caring and others cruel?"

3. Make a list of people who have proved worthy of your trust, and another of people who have proved untrustworthy. What do you notice as you compare the two lists?

Questions to Ponder

1. Think about times when you have been overly gullible. What caused you to feel that way? What's changed?

2. Have there been times in your life when you lost and regained trust in someone? What was that like? What part does forgiveness play in trust?

3. Have you ever continued a relationship with someone you couldn't trust? How did you make that safe for you?

4. Have you ever betrayed someone's trust? Were you able to reestablish the relationship?

5. What can be trusted in your life? What will sustain you? What do you really need in order to live?

Most people have several folks in their lives who have taught them important lessons about trust, both positive and negative. Think about some of those teachers and what they taught you. Choose one teacher of trust you are willing to talk about in the group.

~

GATHERING

Candle Lighting

East: Brother Fire, we invoke warmth. May our hearts be open to each other.

South: Father Air, we invoke inspiration. May our words be wise and kind.

West: Sister Water, we invoke the flow of life. May we have courage.

North: Mother Earth, we invoke groundedness. May we all be here in spirit as well as in body.

Leader: Spirit within, we invoke depth. May we remember all we value.

On Our Hearts   10 minutes

Silence   3 minutes

Shared Readings

In doubt a man of worth will trust to his own wisdom.
    —J.R.R. Tolkien

When you are aware of what you are doing, placing your trust in someone or something takes a lot of courage. It's an act of bravery. It acknowledges that you are not alone in the world and that there is a connection between you and all things.
    —Angel Kyodod William

The best way to make people trustworthy is to trust them.
—Ernest Hemingway

I argue there are two ways for the heart to break: APART into many shards, like a fragment grenade, or OPEN into greater capacity so we can hold life's inevitable tensions creatively, not destructively. Many of us learn how to hold personal tensions in that open, life-giving way.
—Parker Palmer

Trust men, and they will be true to you; treat them greatly, and they will show themselves great.
—Ralph Waldo Emerson

Sharing   45 minutes

Closing Activity   15 minutes

Closing Words

You know that the flower bends when the wind wants it to, and you must become like that—that is, filled with deep trust.
—Rainer Maria Rilke

Song

Announcements

Discussion of Candle Lighting/Extinguishing

Extinguishing the Candle

East: Brother Fire, thank you for warming our hearts.

South: Father Air, we thank you for inspiring us here.

West: Sister Water, thank you for the courage to be present to the flow of life.

North: Mother Earth, we thank you for grounding us here.

Leader: Spirit within, we take you with us to cherish until we meet again.

Spiritual Experiences

BEFORE YOU GATHER

All of us are potentially contemplative. What may be called a "contemplative experience" is natural and common to most of us, at least once in awhile. We are struck dumb by massive shafts of sunlight breaking through dark thunderclouds, falling on the desert. A sleeping child on our lap makes us completely still and fills us with utter peace. In a moment of extreme suffering, something opens up and we somehow know that even though everything is "wrong," everything is really all right. A confrontation with someone who loves us leads us to quiet, deep, honest surrender. In one way or another, we find our way into stillness, quiet, a full emptiness; we open to a place within that is truthful, grounded, humble, and utterly real.

—Brian C. Taylor

In spontaneously occurring unitive experiences, one feels suddenly "swept up" by life, "caught" in a suspended moment where time seems to stand still and awareness peaks in both of its dimensions, becoming at once totally wide awake and open. Everything in the immediate environment is experienced with awesome clarity, and the vast panorama of consciousness lies open. For the duration of the experience—which is usually not long—mental activity seems to be suspended. Preoccupations, misgivings, worries, and desires all seem to evaporate, leaving everything "perfect, just as it is." Usually there are some reactive feelings that occur toward the end of the experience, feelings such as awe, wonder, expansiveness, freedom, warmth, love, and a sense of total truth or "rightness." After the experience is over, there is an almost invariable recollection of having been *at one*.

—Gerald May

Consider This

What is a spiritual experience? William James, the classic American author on this subject, said a hundred years ago that such experiences have four characteristics:

- They are hard to describe.
- The person who has one learns something or knows something about life after the experience that they didn't know, or didn't know so powerfully, before.
- They are relatively brief, discrete experiences, which fade. Nobody experiences this state continuously.
- These experiences come as a gift that we cannot control by any activity of our own. They just happen to us, mostly unexpectedly.

James attached no particular theology or denomination to his description of spiritual experiences, but most religious people would say that these were experiences of God or of the spirit world. However, non-theists also speak of spiritual experiences. Buddhists (who believe that we live in a world of illusions) see them as fleeting gifts of insight into how things really are. Humanists have experiences of oneness, sometimes called "peak experiences," and those who think scientifically point out that science is beginning to find this apprehension of unity and purpose in its disciplines. How you name and explain these experiences is not nearly as important as how you pay attention to them and incorporate them into your understanding of life.

Spiritual experiences can come in meditation, in nature, or in unexpected and unsought moments. They come during extreme situations such as combat and childbirth, and they come during ordinary camping trips, subway travels, and family moments. Sometimes they come in religious services, but so rarely that it is better to think of worship as a training ground for spirituality rather than a playing field. Uncomfortable as it might make us to consider this, there are clear channels between our spiritual and sexual natures, which are remarked upon throughout the world's histories and cultures. These experiences, of oneness, harmony, okay-ness, insight, and joy, have been found by researchers across the human community to be nearly universal. Almost everyone has had such an experience, although it often takes some effort to remember it. (Anything that is hard to describe is hard to remember.) These experiences seem to come disproportionately during difficult times in life, bringing a gift of insight or peace which eases the difficulty.

Sometimes these experiences come with a felt presence, a voice, or a vision. This seems more likely to happen to teens and young adults, and if their religious and cultural education has not equipped them to expect and welcome such experiences, they may be bemused or even frightened by them—or they may take themselves and their experiences to religious communities that will honor and explain them. However, such experiences also come in a more impersonal way, bringing an especially vivid sense of the beauty, connectedness, or pathos of a situation. Humanistic psychologist Abraham Maslow called them "peak experiences."

Maybe something like this has happened to you: You've got a bunch of really pressing problems, and you've tied yourself into knots of anxiety. Desperate for relief, perspective, and a change, you take a walk in a large park. You stump along for an hour, rehearsing your options, your anxieties, your angers and fears, and finally drop into an exhausted inner silence. You mount the crest of a hill and see, down the path, close enough that you can see their beautiful eyes, a family of deer. You come to a startled halt, and for one moment, every fiber of your being is simply present in the moment. The deer look at you, you look at them. A smile plays on your lips, perhaps the first smile in days. A weight drops from your shoulders, and you watch in wonder, feeling somehow deeply related to the deer and their peaceful ways. The deer amble off. You resume your walk, but it's all different now. The weight is gone, the anger, the anxiety. You find yourself thinking, "It's going to be all right. Whatever happens, it will be all right." There's no logical reason for you to think this; your problems are just as dire as they were an hour before. But you have no doubt of this larger wisdom, and so the most important part of your problem, which is your reactivity to your problem, has changed, and you are content to simply do what seems best and await the outcome.

If you believe in the sort of God who answers prayers, you'll tell yourself that all that anxious outpouring on the path was a sort of prayer, and that it has been answered, not by fixing the problems, but by adjusting you. If you believe that grace abounds in the universe, you might think of this as an experience of grace. If you relate to Native American wisdom, you might think of the deer as spirits sent to share their wisdom with you. If you think psychologically, you'll tell yourself that coming so abruptly across the deer startled you out of your addictive anxiety rehearsal and reminded you of the larger life that includes them, and that experience helped you to get on with your life. If you don't have words or concepts for an experience like that, you'll still have it and benefit from it, but you will probably forget it. Since it is not likely to happen again soon, forgetting will deprive you of its continuing benefits.

Or maybe what happens to you is something like this: Some time after the death of a loved one, you have the sense of their presence and a chance to say good-bye. Or the night stars remind you of the infinity of the universe, and you find yourself feeling both minuscule and unified with the All at the same time. Or you are part of a group of people working hard together to triumph over some injustice, and the joy you feel is larger than the triumph. "The arc of the universe," you think. "We are bending the arc of the universe." Or, recovering from surgery, you are sitting by a sunny window, feeling suffused not only with sunlight, but with joy.

Religious liberalism authorizes individuals (rather than a tradition, a book, or a hierarchy) to come to their own beliefs by examining their minds, hearts, and experiences. That means that religious liberals, even more than other religious people, should pay attention to their spiritual experiences and ponder their messages, even when they can't be explained. Spiritual experiences are moments of mystery and wonder, after all, not equations on a math test. The point is not to explain and solve. The point is to appreciate and learn, asking yourself what kinds of meanings the experience could give to your life, and to follow those clues ruthlessly, even into uncomfortable territory. Freedom is not for the timid.

The first step in honoring spiritual experiences is to remember them and save them, usually by writing them down. If you think you don't have spiritual experiences, write about any special moments. When was the last time something happened that left tears in your eyes or a catch in your voice? When emotion wells up in us, it is always pointing us toward what is most important. Do you remember unusually peaceful moments, in nature or anywhere else? Times when you felt "in the flow" and in harmony with your surroundings? Not all of those experiences are the sort of thing William James or Abraham Maslow wrote about, but they point us in the same directions, and if we honor them, we send a message to our psyche that we'd like to remember or experience more things like that.

It often takes courage to share our spiritual experiences, and we want to feel safe when we tell others about these fleeting, numinous, hard-to-interpret experiences. Just hearing ourselves tell these stories is often useful as we incorporate them into our lives; it helps us ask ourselves how they fit, or don't, with what we believe. Our spiritual and peak experiences can be major forces that induce us to grow in faith, if only we take them seriously and follow up the clues they give us about the depth of our lives.

Activities

1. Take a few minutes to think about any spiritual or peak experiences you have had. Where did they take place? Were you alone or with others? What else was going on in your life at the time? What kinds of feelings were you left with? What kind of messages did you receive? Did you learn anything? Now create a picture of yourself in these settings, using cut-up magazine pictures, drawing, or whatever medium works best for you. Or, if you'd rather, write a paragraph about it.

2. Think of a symbol or memento of the experience identified in the first activity which you can use to remind yourself about it. Rocks, photographs, drawings, figurines, and candles are all time-honored items used for this purpose.

3. Look again at William James's characteristics of a spiritual experience on page 40. Create a haiku that describes a spiritual experience you have had, incorporating as many of the four characteristics as you can. A haiku is a poem of three lines with five syllables in the first line, seven syllables in the second line, and five syllables in the last. You may want to title it. Here are two examples:

The Sistine Chapel
God reaches to man,
Then Buddha, and a Druid.
Aha, my world shifts.
    —Alicia Hawkins

Waves crashing, black sands.
In awe of powerful Earth,
Feeling peaceful, strong.
    —Grace Perce

Questions to Ponder

1. What has been your most powerful spiritual experience? Perhaps it was out in nature, perhaps a sudden realization or a coincidence so improbable that you were startled out of taking the world for granted.

2. When do you feel you have been in the presence of the Holy? When have you been awed or moved to tears? What have been your experiences of profound peace or "at-one-ment"?

3. Many of us are spiritually shy. What makes it hard to speak about the ways you connect with the sacred?

4. If none of this rings any bells with you, think about high points and peak experiences of your life.

Think about a powerful spiritual experience you are willing to share. Decide on a symbol to remind you of this experience and bring it to the gathering to help you tell your story.

∾

GATHERING

Candle Lighting

East: Brother Fire, we invoke warmth. May our hearts be open to each other.

South: Father Air, we invoke inspiration. May our words be wise and kind.

West: Sister Water, we invoke the flow of life. May we have courage.

North: Mother Earth, we invoke groundedness. May we all be here in spirit as well as in body.

Leader: Spirit within, we invoke depth. May we remember all we value.

On Our Hearts   10 minutes

Silence   3 minutes

Shared Readings

Many who have described mystical experiences, particularly in nature, repeatedly remark upon "seeing things more clearly than ever seen before," or "When I see this way, I see truly," or of "seeing something as it truly was."
   —Carl Von Essen

The evidence largely supports the view that mystical experience takes two forms, one a realization of the unity of all things, the other of the divine presence. Both forms of experience can be accompanied by an awareness of light, which can have the effect of appearing to transform the surroundings.
   —Davie Fontana

I experienced the sense of connection I was seeking in those moments when the veil between worlds lifted, in those thin places where I could feel the presence of the divine.
   —Ann Armbrecht

Anyone who has had an experience of mystery knows that there is a dimension of the universe that is not that which is available to his senses. There is a pertinent saying in one of the Upanishads:

"When before the beauty of a sunset or of a mountain you pause and exclaim, 'Ah,' you are participating in divinity."
—Joseph Campbell

Sharing   60 minutes

Closing Activity

Closing Words

According to the Kabbalah, at some point in the beginning of things, the Holy was broken up into countless sparks, which were scattered throughout the universe. There is a god spark in everyone and in everything, a sort of diaspora of goodness. God's immanent presence among us is encountered daily in the most simple, humble, and ordinary ways. The Kabbalah teaches that the Holy may speak to you from its many hidden places at any time. The world may whisper in your ear, or the spark of God in you may whisper in your heart.
—Rachel Naomi Remen

Song

Announcements

Extinguishing the Candle

East: Brother Fire, thank you for warming our hearts.
South: Father Air, we thank you for inspiring us here.
West: Sister Water, thank you for the courage to be present to the flow of life.

North: Mother Earth, we thank you for grounding us here.

Leader: Spirit within, we take you with us to cherish until we meet again.

Addiction

∿

BEFORE YOU GATHER

At some point in their lives (often quite young) these sensitive souls stumble across something that makes them feel better. For some it's alcohol; for others it's sugar, drugs, shopping, sex, work, gambling, or some other substance or activity that hits the spot. "Ahh," they sigh, "I've found what's been missing. This is the answer to my problems." They have discovered a new best friend—their drug of choice.
—B.J. Gallagher

The call to metanoia, transformation, and repentance comes to us in different ways. Yet we must all at some moment "hit bottom" and vow to change our lives. The "ego" crashes and the I AM, a light greater than the ego, breaks through the isolation and separation we have created. If the fall into ego lies on one side of the call, the vow to selflessness lies on the other. Such a vow is not made once but must be renewed with every breath.
—Christopher Bamford

Americans are variously addicted to many things, among them wealth, sex, food, work, alcohol, caffeine and tobacco. By attacking addiction in others, we can feel good about ourselves without coming to any insight about our own addictions.
—Walter Wink

Consider This

For many of us, "addictions" are things that other people struggle with; sometimes we're aware of them because others' addictions have given us pain. Others of us are all too aware of our addictions. We're in twelve-step groups, we keep struggling to avoid the thing we are addicted to, and we know the pain our addictions cause ourselves and those around us. Whether those addictions are life threatening, as alcohol addiction often is, or simply bemusing, such as a need for caffeine in the morning, almost all of us have noticed that there are some things that we "have" to have or we just don't feel right.

The reason we don't feel right if we've not had our afternoon Coke or our morning smoke or our evening sex is that our body has become habituated to the stimulus. It actually anticipates our activity by changing the mix of hormones and neurotransmitters that bathes our bodies in anticipation of "the fix." If the fix goes missing, our body has to backtrack to re-regulate our metabolism, and in the meantime, we're sleepy or agitated or otherwise don't feel right. Our clever body's attempt to stay on top of things has backfired, and that's so uncomfortable that many feedback loops are put in place to make this habit pleasurable so that we just won't skip it. Whether the habit is an afternoon tennis game or an afternoon candy bar, nose drops or heroin, the mechanism is the same.

It is not just substances that can kick-start these dynamics. Most of us are in some ways addicted to the high levels of stress in our lives, and many of us have to re-create that stress even on vacation in order to feel good. Some people "have" to gamble, some "have" to shop, and others are so habituated to the adrenaline high of sports that missing that weekly experience makes them feel cranky and distracted.

The mechanisms which drive all these addictions are the same, though their consequences in our lives are very different. Needing a Coke in your hand to keep up your creative edge in the afternoon is not as big a problem for most people as needing to smoke, and the addiction to a runner's high is usually healthier than needing to feel empty and pure inside by purging or starving yourself.

Some addictions leave us a bit of flexibility—if there's no Coke, we can manage with a bottle of water and keep working with a bit of grumbling. Other addictions seem to take our freedom entirely away from us and we just "have" to have whatever it is, no matter the consequences.

Our culture has generally reserved the word *addict* for a person whose life is falling apart, the victim of one or more of a fairly small range of addictions, including illegal drugs, alcohol, sex, and food. Most people do not think of themselves as addicted to anything, and use words like *habits, routines,* and *problems* to describe what actually are addictions. Admitting to ourselves that almost everybody has some addictions, including us, opens the possibility of compassion for others and gives us some tools to understand our lives and remain as free as possible from addictions.

There are a number of signals that a habit has become an addiction, and first among them is the sense that we're no longer completely free in relationship to this habit. A glass of wine in the evening is downright healthy, they say, but if we find that we can't enjoy the evening without one, or if we find ourselves slipping and sliding to the liquor store in a raging snowstorm, cursing all the way, we have to realize we are really not free in this part of our lives.

Other signs that our ways have become addictions include increasing tolerance to the substance/mood/behavior, meaning that you need more of it to feel right than you did before. One drink becomes two, an occasional dessert becomes a nightly dessert, a few minutes of computer games before bedtime becomes a nightly game session into the wee hours.

Third, we experience withdrawal symptoms if we can't have our fix of whatever we're addicted to. These symptoms range from the "I didn't have my coffee yet" headache through uneasiness to the full-blown DTs. If there are absolutely no consequences from not engaging in our "addictive" behavior, it's probably not really an addiction. (This is one of the ways we can sort out whether we just really enjoy something, like surfing the web or sex, or whether we are really addicted.)

Finally, addictions do a number on our psyche. They distort our attention, focusing it on the addiction. The gambler who leaves his children asleep in his parked car is suffering from hijacked attention. Addictions also cause us to engage in all manner of self-deceptions. The alcoholic believes, at first, that "everybody" drinks this much. The stressaholic believes that this much stress won't hurt her. The society that is addicted to oil simply reasons that global warming isn't real. In this self-deceptive haze, we're liable to hurt others and resist healing for ourselves.

One of the most painful parts of confronting our addictions is deeply realizing that we are not as free as we wish we were. We don't have the power to put down the cookie or not check our Facebook page. We want not to need these things, but we don't seem able to control what we want, or even—and this is a humbling experience to anyone who faces it—how we act.

It's small comfort to remember that craving is deeply a part of who we humans are, but we have to accept this to begin to work with it. Self-hatred only adds to our problems. We're genetically programmed to crave things that increase the survival of our genes, and through most of human history, there were so few material comforts and intoxicants, and so much work to do, that no braking mechanism was needed. If you imbibed alcohol only when the fruit was overripe and overate only a couple of times a year, there was no evolutionary need to restrain your addiction. Some people would go even further than that. They would say that craving, the desire to have more than we have, to know more than we know, to do more than we have done, is what makes humans different from animals. Our addictions are not just problematic, they are fundamental. And while they limit our freedom, they are also a pathway into the spiritual life; they allow us to relate to others and find compassion in ourselves for ourselves and others.

The situation is ironic: We are human because of our cravings, yet our cravings reduce the freedom that makes us human. So a frontal attack on the problem of excessive cravings simply won't work. We have to resort to a more mystical understanding of the situation and be gentle with ourselves and others. When we realize that some activity, mood, or substance in our lives has become a problem, but that we don't seem to be able to just stop, we will have to take a more holistic approach, acknowledging the courage it takes to tackle even modest addictions. We will reduce our temptation load while we explore what this addiction means to us, what we're using it for, how we might replace it with healthier ways, and whether we want to engage the help of others or God to help us out of this particular hole.

By and large, we can't treat addictions as if they were ordinary problems in our lives. They go much deeper than that. Carl Jung was the first to note that at heart, addictions are a spiritual (deep) problem. Remembering that "spirits" was an old word for alcohol, his formula was, "Combat spirits with spirituality." That, of course, is the process of twelve-step programs, which are the only widely effective treatment for life-threatening and life-limiting addictions. By putting people ready to deal with their addictions on a spiritual path, these programs help them access resources of faith, community, and inner strength.

Whatever your addictions and however strong their grip on you, self-knowledge is the beginning of freedom.

Activities

1. List habitual behaviors in your life that seem to be addictions. See if they fit the following criteria:

   Increasing tolerance (the amount needed to achieve the effect increases)
   Withdrawal symptoms (for example, irritability when the Internet is down)
   Self-deception
   Loss of will power
   Distortion of our attention

There are many examples of addictions in the essay. Here are several more:

Spending money
Power/control
Worry/stress
Television
Being with other people
Staying connected (cell phones, email, social networking)
Playing computer games
Being thin or muscled
Eating salt, fat, carbohydrates, sugar
Sports
Busy-ness
Big houses, cars
Adventure
Love
Religion
Success
Travel

2. Here is a psalm adapted to speak about the struggle to overcome addiction. Try writing your own psalm.

Save me, O God,
I have gotten myself in deep waters
and find no firm ground under my feet.
I am tired of crying.
I feel at war with myself and with others;
I'm unable to do what is expected of me.

O God, you know my foolishness and my faults—
do you love me anyway?
I really am sinking.
These rushing, dark waters are going to swallow me up.

Answer me, God!
Your loving kindness would save me.
If I could see your face, it would be enough
to ease my distress and help me relax in the flood.

I will remember that you are here,
even in the torrent, even in the war.
I will give thanks for the small beauties
and kindnesses of the day
and for the love that is in my heart.
　　　—Psalm 69, adapted by Christine Robinson

Questions to Ponder

1. What addictions have you dealt with in the past?

2. What is an addiction you are considering dealing with in your life? What tactics might you use to be successful?

3. Describe some addictions that don't ruin your life, but you don't seem to be able to stop.

4. Are there some addictions that you're okay with allowing to continue?

5. Are there ways that your addictions play a positive role in your life? Is the role completely positive?

Look at the list of addictive behaviors in your life. Decide which ones you are willing to share with the group and how you will do that.

GATHERING

Candle Lighting

East: Brother Fire, we invoke warmth. May our hearts be open to each other.

South: Father Air, we invoke inspiration. May our words be wise and kind.

West: Sister Water, we invoke the flow of life. May we have courage.

North: Mother Earth, we invoke groundedness. May we all be here in spirit as well as in body.

Leader: Spirit within, we invoke depth. May we remember all we value.

On Our Hearts   10 minutes

Silence   3 minutes

Shared Readings

We use all kinds of ways to escape—all addictions stem from this moment when we meet our edge and we just can't stand it. We feel we have to soften it, pad it with something, and we become addicted to whatever it is that seems to ease the pain.
  —Pema Chödrön

One trait of members of addictive families is [that] we never recognize our own addictions.
  —Lorna Luft

Habits are first cobwebs, then cables.
—Spanish proverb

Are we all addicted to something? And if we are, does this lessen the impact of "addiction" in our lives or does it reflect something about what we are seeking and not finding? Buddhist thought suggests that the human condition of life is incomplete and unfulfilled and our craving leads us to suffering.
—Carolyn Brown

Every form of addiction is bad, no matter whether the narcotic be alcohol or morphine or idealism.
—Carl Jung

Sharing   60 minutes

Closing Activity

Closing Words

That which is worthy of doing, create with your hands.
That which is worthy of repeating, speak with a clear voice.
That which is worthy of remembering, hold in your hearts.
And that which is worthy of living, go and live it now.
—Steve J. Crump

Song

Announcements

Extinguishing the Candle

East: Brother Fire, thank you for warming our hearts.

South: Father Air, we thank you for inspiring us here.

West: Sister Water, thank you for the courage to be present to the flow of life.

North: Mother Earth, we thank you for grounding us here.

Leader: Spirit within, we take you with us to cherish until we meet again.

Calling

∾

BEFORE YOU GATHER

Discovering vocation does not mean scrambling toward some prize just beyond my reach but accepting the treasure of true self I already possess. Vocation does not come from a voice "out there" calling me to become something I am not. It comes from a voice "in here" calling me to be the person I was born to be, to fulfill the original selfhood given me at birth by God.
   —Parker J. Palmer

Tell me, what is it you plan to do
with your one wild and precious life?
   —Mary Oliver

If the call is without beginning, it is also without end. Every call seems to lie at the intersection of past and future. From one direction, it echoes up through time and memory from our source and origin, defining who we are, alerting us to whom we shall become. From the other, it comes toward us as destiny, drawing us toward an ineffable goal. You might say that to live is itself to be called. Perhaps that is why one of the meanings of anthropos, or human being, is "to look up," as one looks up when one hears one's name called.
   —Christopher Bamford

Before his death, Rabbi Zusya said, "In the coming world, they will not ask me, 'Why were you not Moses?' They will ask me, 'Why were you not Zusya?'"

—Folk tale

Consider This

In one of the world's classic "calling" stories, God tells his prophet Jonah to leave Palestine, go to the next country over, and tell the people there to mend their ways. Jonah hears the message loud and clear and knows that he should obey, but he doesn't want to go. So he sets sail in the opposite direction. God turns him around with a big storm, which is how he ends up in the belly of that whale. The whale spits him out on shore, and this time, he does as he is told.

Taken metaphorically, this story reminds us that when we become aware that there is something we are supposed to do, it is downright dangerous to resist. Lots of psychologists would agree. They see clients who are stuck in a dark place—a metaphorical belly of a whale—because they can't bring themselves to follow their dream or their calling. Interestingly, researchers in unexplained remissions of usually fatal diseases often hear this story: "I was told I had a year to live, so I decided that I'd ditch my job and learn to (paint, fly, fish), which I've been wanting to do all my life. And I'm still alive." The sense that we are doing what we are supposed to be doing in life is one of the most satisfying feelings we can have, even when the work is hard or the conditions rough.

The prophet Isaiah tells another classic calling story. He has a vision of the world in misery and hears God asking, "Whom shall I send?" His first reaction is that he is utterly unworthy, but when this passes, his head clears, and he finds himself saying, "Here am I. Send me." His subsequent life is not easy, but it shines with purpose and meaning.

Those words, "Here am I. Send me," resonate in the hearts of many people who have sensed a call to a difficult task and have decided to undertake it. Whether it is parenting a child, ending slavery in the United States, starting a new faith, or saving a neighborhood awash in industrial waste, when you ask people why they are doing these tasks, they say things like, "It needed doing," and "I just had to," and "There was no one else." Calling, and its related word, *vocation* (which comes from the Latin *vocare*, to call), have pretentious overtones to many. People are reluctant to use these words because they imply a divine sanction that doesn't seem appropriate —or people think they will be teased for using that terminology. Some of this reluctance is appropriate. There is hardly anything more dangerous than an inflated ego combined with the sense that one is especially chosen to do God's will! (Most prophets begin their careers protesting their unworthiness.) In spite of abuses of this word *called*, which range from the tedious to the horrific, it's just too useful to do without. Most people at times sense that they are supposed to be doing something in their lives beyond what is easy or comfortable, and find that, when they do it, their sense of fulfillment is its own reward. That's a vocation, a calling.

The world's religious and secular literature is replete with descriptions of calling and vocation, both dramatic (Jonah's whale) and subtle. Sometimes a call develops slowly and organically in a person's life with no particular drama. As something they feel drawn to increases in importance, they gain skills and get good feedback from others; their call is validated by those around them and by their own sense of the rightness of what they are about. Sometimes a call seems to come quite suddenly or involves a real turnaround, surprising the person feeling the call even more than it surprises onlookers. There are times when a call seems to come from outside; a person actually hears a voice or feels directed from without in a very vivid way. More often, a calling comes from inside, and the person feels that this is their deep wisdom surfacing.

How do we know we've found our real calling and are not just indulging in wishful thinking? That difficult question has been answered in different ways over the years. Fredrick Buechner's famous words remind us that our calling can be found at the place "where your deep gladness and the world's deep hunger meet." Our calling is much bigger than our individual preference. Howard Thurman, African-American writer, minister, and college chaplain had a more mystical sense of calling. "Don't ask yourself what the world needs," he wrote, "ask yourself what makes you come alive, and then go and do that because that's what the world needs, people who have come alive." Taking this route to discovering call requires trusting a deep and positive connection between your life and the world's life. Whose advice should you follow? One possibility is to follow what seems like the least comfortable path. For instance, people who are serious and other-focused by nature might need to work hard at discerning what makes them come alive, while those who have always followed their own drummer might take Buechner's tactic of looking for which of the world's deep hungers most moves them.

The work of discerning calling is continuous. Older teens and young adults struggle with calling and vocation as they decide on college and career direction. In a few years, they will begin to ask themselves about partners and children. Midlife brings up questions of call again for many people, as the first career chosen no longer seems quite right, or the children grow up and leave home. For most people, retirement is not a matter of leaving the world, or even the paid workforce, but about discerning another calling, asking, "What am I supposed to do with my sixties and seventies, while I still have energy to give the world?"

Nor is finding a calling appropriate only for our biggest decisions about vocation, family, and demanding long-term projects. A sense of calling comes big and small. We may feel called to leave academia and join the Peace Corps, but we might also feel called to pick up litter on a hiking trail. When a child falls from his bicycle in the street, many people will feel called to give assistance for a few moments. If that child is orphaned, someone in the family or outside of it may feel that their vocation is to raise him. A few people feel an intense call to long-term, huge projects such as world peace or child welfare reform, but many more will be nudged by a sense of calling to work for a candidate for elected office for a season, to start a chess club and teen center, or to advocate one day a week for a child in foster care. A few find that their love for congregations and parishioners nudges them into ordained ministry. More discover enormous satisfaction in participating in their congregation's ministries: They visit the dying, serve meals to the homeless, sweat over the budget or the building plans, or serve at worship. "This is what I'm supposed to be doing," they say. "It's my calling."

We do plenty of important things in our lives that don't feel like a calling, some of them big things. "I never really felt a call to be a parent," we might say, "but then I fell in love with a parent, and that made me a parent, too. So I did it. I think I did a good job. And I'm glad she's grown up and is doing so well." Similarly, there are those who serve in the military because they like the structured life, the paycheck, or the job training, and this doesn't subtract from their service one whit. We should always be proud of doing a good job where a good job needs doing. Feeling a calling adds extra satisfaction to a life, but tending to our responsibilities is always the calling beneath the call. When our responsibilities seem to conflict with our sense of call, we have to discern how to proceed so that we can find ways to fulfill both, because it is almost always the case, in the end, that our true calling and our true responsibilities are deeply related. The reluctant stepparent was called by love (for the spouse) into that relationship. The soldier whose main motivation to enlist was to better her opportunities was called to self-development by her deepest inner self. One way or another, we move through life by negotiating and balancing our longings and our responsibilities, the world's needs and our joy.

Activities

1. Answer the questions below with a list of words or phrases.

   - What activities bring you joy? What ones energize you?
   - What comes easily to you, or is effortless?
   - What activities cause you to lose track of time when you're doing them?

- What do other people say is your strength?
- What are you really passionate about?

On a sheet of paper draw a large circle. Write the words inside the circle, combining some that seem related.

Draw boundaries around the words or groups of words, indicating the relative size or importance of these activities in your life. For instance, if one activity feels more important than the others, the boundary around it will take up more space inside the circle than the others.

Reflect on your circle for some clues as to your calling.

For example, your circle might look like this:

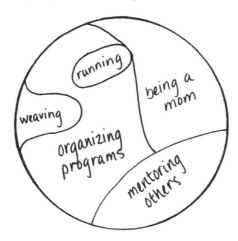

2. You can do this as a writing exercise or you can make a collage or drawing. Divide a piece of paper in half. On the right side, list or draw the world's needs. On the left, write or draw your gifts and gladness. Now, start drawing lines to show intersections between the world's needs and your gifts or desires.

Questions to Ponder

1. What are your greatest joys, gifts, memories? When did you feel the satisfaction of responding to a calling in the past?

2. What do you want to do in the future? Could you earn a living at it?

3. What needs of the world leap out at you? What issues are dearest to your heart? What do you see that others miss?

4. How did your parents respect their calling, or not?

5. In what way do you practice your calling at work, in volunteer activities, or in your relationships with family and friends?

6. What calls in your life have you run away from or been unable to follow?

7. If you had a year to live, what would you do?

Complete Activity 1. Think of what you are willing to share about the qualities and descriptions of your true self.

∼

GATHERING

Candle Lighting

East: Brother Fire, we invoke warmth. May our hearts be open to each other.

South: Father Air, we invoke inspiration. May our words be wise and kind.

West: Sister Water, we invoke the flow of life. May we have courage.

North: Mother Earth, we invoke groundedness. May we all be here in spirit as well as in body.

Leader: Spirit within, we invoke depth. May we remember all we value.

On Our Hearts   10 minutes

Silence   3 minutes

Shared Readings

Silence has taught me: Our lives are usable for God. We need not be effective, but only transparent and vulnerable.
     —Richard Rohr

Our strongest gifts are usually those we are barely aware of possessing. They are a part of our God-given nature, with us from the moment we drew first breath, and we are no more conscious of having them than we are of breathing.
     —Parker J. Palmer

Do what you can—and the task will rest lightly in your hand, so lightly that you will be able to look forward to the more difficult tests which may be awaiting you.
     —Dag Hammarskjöld

The future enters into us . . . in order to transform itself in us long before it happens.
     —Rainer Maria Rilke

I wonder where my life is, the one that could
Have been and never was, the daring one . . .
     —Jorge Luis Borges

We must be willing to get rid of the life we've planned, so as to have the life that is waiting for us.

—Joseph Campbell

Sharing   60 minutes

Closing Activity

Closing Words

Great ideas, it has been said, come into the world as gently as doves. Perhaps, then, if we listen attentively, we shall hear amid the uproar of empires and nations, a faint flutter of wings, a gentle stirring of life and hope.

Some will say that this hope lies in a nation; others, in a man. I believe rather that it is awakened, revived, nourished by millions of solitary individuals whose deeds and works every day negate frontiers and the crudest implications of history.

As a result, there shines forth fleetingly the ever-threatened truth that each and every man, on the foundation of his own sufferings and joys, builds for all.

—Albert Camus

Song

Announcements

Extinguishing the Candle

East: Brother Fire, thank you for warming our hearts.
South: Father Air, we thank you for inspiring us here.

West: Sister Water, thank you for the courage to be present to the flow of life.

North: Mother Earth, we thank you for grounding us here.

Leader: Spirit within, we take you with us to cherish until we meet again.

Shadow

∾

BEFORE YOU GATHER

The simplest, most functional definition of the Shadow is that which renders us uncomfortable with ourselves.
—James Hollis

To confront a person with his shadow is to show him his own light. Once one has experienced a few times what it is like to stand judgingly between the opposites, one begins to understand what is meant by the self. Anyone who perceives his shadow and his light simultaneously sees himself from two sides and thus gets in the middle.
—Carl Jung

Unconsciously, we launch onto others those impulses and traits that we ourselves have but cannot accept. When we do not own or deal with these impulses and traits (our shadow), we are forced to act them out through projection or other means.
—Sheryl Towers

Some of the pure gold of our personality is relegated to the shadow because it can find no place in that great leveling process that is culture.
—Robert A. Johnson

Consider This

Each of us has a self that we present to the world, a set of traits which we have accepted or chosen, developed or learned. Many of these traits we were required to develop by our parents and society —we learned a certain level of neatness, a particular kind of manners, perseverance, sex roles, aggressiveness, nurturing, and so on. Some traits we seem innately bound to develop, and we pursue them whether or not we are forced or encouraged to do so. One way or another, out of all the possibilities of life, we focus on a few traits. We are quiet or loud, intellectual or physical, introverted or extroverted, nurturing or aloof. We have developed our musical talent, and we have decided not to let our anger show. All this makes up a unique personality. We tend to think of ourselves as being that personality, but our public persona is only one part of ourselves.

The other part resides in the unconscious, and it consists of all of the traits we have not developed, including ones we would not like to express. This is the shadow side of ourselves, and it is just as important to us as the persona we present to the world. Our shadow might contain the artistic side we were not allowed to develop, the dreaminess we consider to be at odds with success, the love of nature which we have repressed since childhood, the anger which was not acceptable in our family. It might include a talent for math that has never really been needed, racial stereotypes that we know are not acceptable, and a whiny child who always wants her own way. Our shadow, like our public persona, has its strengths and weaknesses; the mirror opposites of the face we present to the world.

Some children are rigidly socialized into a particular mold. They are told, "Boys don't cry." "We hope and expect that you will go into the family business." "You can choose soccer or basketball, but you have to play a sport." "You may not yell, no matter how excited you are." Children mostly take these instructions very seriously. They want to comply with expectations. If some expectations run contrary to their own desires or inclinations, they have to work hard to keep their shadow side from asserting itself. This can make such children rigid and cautious. Other children are raised more freely—gender roles are less rigid, feelings are expressed more openly, children are free to dream of many careers and develop the skills and traits they need. These children will also have a shadow, for they too will choose to develop one set of traits and skills and leave others behind. However, they will probably live a little more easily with that shadow.

No one really likes to be told they have a shadow within. We try to hide it from others and ourselves; most of us do this not just by controlling its outbursts, which is appropriate and necessary, but also by denying its existence, which is not such a smart move because that only makes the shadow stronger. Understanding the nature and development of our shadow is an important part of healthy self-acceptance as well as healthy self-control.

Obviously, we can't cut open a person's skull and find a shadow, but its existence can be inferred from many sources. We have become accustomed to the notion that even the meekest and mildest persons can commit terrible crimes. We are no longer surprised when an accused person's neighbors claim that he or she was quiet and docile. On the more positive side, we're familiar with the story of the basically passive, shy person who in an emergency becomes a leader and afterward continually wonders where that strength came from. The answer is that we all have many possibilities hidden within us.

Our culture implicitly acknowledges this inner reality in many ways. From *Moby-Dick* to *Star Trek*, from comic-book superheroes to Jekyll and Hyde, shadow selves are a common feature of our art, literature, and culture. The opportunity to play with our shadow is what makes Halloween fun. We laugh at Freudian slips because we know they mean a great deal; they are the momentary play of the shadow, and they tell us something about ourselves and what we are really feeling.

Parents often project their shadows onto their children. This is why conventional wisdom says that preachers' kids are hell-raisers.

The old-time preacher had to be upright, proper, quiet, and loving in all things, and therefore had a shadow of rebellious, mischievous, selfish qualities, which his children were only too happy to act out.

Individuals clearly have a shadow, and it seems that groups of people do, too. This shadow is often projected onto other groups, so that qualities that are repressed in one culture are seen to be overly expressed in another, often without any basis in reality. This can result in the worst kinds of prejudice. Consider how the sexually uptight culture of the white American South became obsessed with the perceived sexuality of African-American men, and how the contained cultures of Europe started thinking of noisy, space-loving American tourists as "ugly Americans." Among the benefits of owning our shadow is that we will not feel the need for such self-righteous posturing and will get along better with our neighbors.

It is important to realize that this shadow is not necessarily evil. Rather, it contains all the parts of ourselves that are not in our "up front" personality, all of the strong opposites of our weaknesses and rounded parts of our sharp edges. These shadow qualities sometimes begin to see the light of day in the second half of life, when, having become fairly secure in our self-concept, we can explore other facets of our personality which were too threatening to explore before. The go-getter who becomes more introspective at midlife, the empty nester who develops a passion for graduate school, the widower who discovers that he has a very sociable side are all discovering rich parts of themselves that had, probably for good reasons, been undeveloped. The second half of life would be dull indeed if it were just a matter of forty more years of the "same old same old." The shadow offers riches for the maturing adult to explore.

As we come to know our shadow, embrace our undeveloped side, and bring into our awareness those traits we have decided not to express, we gain the wholeness of self-knowledge and some control we might not otherwise have had.

The best way to get acquainted with your shadow is to think about behaviors and traits in others that drive you crazy. Since the shadow is cast by strong traits in your person—perhaps traits that are a bit too strong and developed—what makes you crazy tells you about what you have hidden. For instance, if you are driven wild by people who are late, then lateness is a part of your shadow. That suggests that you have an extremely well-developed sense of time and perhaps a somewhat rigid belief in the value of time.

Other ways to get to know your shadow are to remember times when you reacted to something in a way you think of as "just not myself." From the Freudian slip to the surprising meltdown, these uncomfortable memories can tell you something about your shadow. Also, consider the Halloween costumes you particularly relish. The sexy barmaid? The big baby? The ugly old hag? The friendly puppy? These might also be clues about your shadow. Finally, consider how you are when you are at your most playful. In most of us, our serious side is our main personality. If we find that when relaxing and fooling around we are drawn to doodling or music, perhaps those are traits which want to see the light of day.

We have to keep our shadow under control to live an ordered life, but that doesn't mean denying its existence or hating to have it ever expressed. Curiosity is a much better attitude toward the shadow than repression. We are more whole and more likely to be happy if we know our shadow and give it some safe space to play.

Activities

1. Make a list of five or six people who bug you or get on your nerves. This list will not be shared in the gathering. Next to each person, list the qualities in them that you most dislike. Be as specific as you can. Consider that those qualities may be some of your shadow aspects.

2. Think forward to a time in your life when you no longer have your present pressures of family and job. Imagine what your

life might include as you let some of the undeveloped aspects of your personality that have been relegated to the shadow emerge. If you have been an academic, you may try something artistic and creative. If you could just fool around all day, what would that look like? Describe what might be included in such a life.

3. Think of costumes you have worn over the years or costumes you've seen others wear. What costume would you wear, if you dared, to an imaginary Shadow Ball? What does that say about you?

4. Make a list of ten qualities that you don't have, characteristics that describe a person who is the opposite of you. These would be descriptions you would deny if someone suggested that they described you.

Questions to Ponder

1. Is there a situation in which you consistently overreact? Could it be that something is hooking into your shadow?

2. Have you made any Freudian slips lately? Do they tell you anything about your shadow?

3. Try writing a dialogue between your conscious self and one of your shadow qualities.

4. What influences helped to shape your shadow? Who or what helped to put those qualities in shadow?

The above exercises should give you some clues about aspects of your shadow. Choose one shadow aspect and bring a simple "costume" to represent it—a piece of clothing, an adornment or accessory, such as a jaunty hat if you are a very contained person, a broom to signify the witch that you are careful not to show, or a shopping list if you are a spontaneous person.

∾

GATHERING

Candle Lighting

East: Brother Fire, we invoke warmth. May our hearts be open to each other.

South: Father Air, we invoke inspiration. May our words be wise and kind.

West: Sister Water, we invoke the flow of life. May we have courage.

North: Mother Earth, we invoke groundedness. May we all be here in spirit as well as in body.

Leader: Spirit within, we invoke depth. May we remember all we value.

On Our Hearts   10 minutes

Guided Meditation   3 minutes

Shared Readings

The Shadow is the landfill of the self. Yet it is also a sort of vault: It holds great, unrealized potentialities within you.
  —Joseph Campbell

The negative feelings that your conscious self holds toward your hidden self have been projected onto that other person. Whenever you find yourself feeling self-righteous, you are in the midst of such a projection.
—Sheldon Kopp

At first glance, the shadow would appear to hold mainly what's negative; in fact, it is holding what is positive hostage. It takes an enormous amount of courage to go down through the shadow material in order to retrieve the essential gift it contains.
—Gail Collins-Ranadive

If we cannot bear to bring our unacknowledged fears of feeling into the light of consciousness we shall continue to need "enemies" onto which we can off-load the suppressed self-hate or fear of being overwhelmed which is simmering below the surface of our lives.
—Jo Farrow

Everything that irritates us about others can lead us to an understanding of ourselves.
—Carl Jung

Sharing   60 minutes

Closing Activity

Closing Words

A soulful life is never without shadow, and some of the soul's power comes from its shadow qualities. If we want to live from our depths—soulfully—then we will have to give up all pretenses to innocence.
—Thomas Moore

Song

Announcements

Extinguishing the Candle

East: Brother Fire, thank you for warming our hearts.

South: Father Air, we thank you for inspiring us here.

West: Sister Water, thank you for the courage to be present to the flow of life.

North: Mother Earth, we thank you for grounding us here.

Leader: Spirit within, we take you with us to cherish until we meet again.

After Death

꩜

BEFORE YOU GATHER

Nothing personal is to remain. We empty ourselves, we surrender, we unfold—until one day our gestures are found in swaying tree-tops and our smile is resurrected among the children who play underneath these trees.
   —Rainer Maria Rilke

I would like to believe when I die that I have given myself away like a tree that sows seeds every spring and never counts the loss, because it is not loss, it is adding to future life. It is the tree's way of being. Strongly rooted perhaps, but spilling out its treasure on the wind.
   —May Sarton

How does one address a mystery? Cautiously—let us go cautiously, then, to the end of our certainty, to the boundary of all we know, to the rim of uncertainty, to the perimeter of the unknown which surrounds us. . . . Simply be in the intimate presence of mystery, unashamed—unadorned—unafraid.
   —Gordon B. McKeeman

[Death is] the undiscovered country from whose bourn no traveler returns.
   —William Shakespeare

For what is it to die but to stand naked in the wind and to melt into the sun?
—Kahlil Gibran

Death is only a launching into the region of the strange Untried; it is but the first salutation to the possibilities of the immense Remote, the Wild, the Watery, the Unshored.
—Herman Melville

Consider This

The Archbishop of Canterbury once said to Bertrand Russell, the celebrated atheist, "I believe in immortality, much more than the evidence warrants." Russell replied, "I disbelieve in immortality much more than the evidence warrants." The two were closer in much of their theologies than it might look on the surface. Both understood that, in spite of the fact that there can be no definitive proof for or against immortality, there are important reasons to make a guess and live out its consequences. The Archbishop's life experience allowed him to trust the Christian religious tradition with its particular beliefs about life after death. It is also possible that he had had mystical experiences which suggested the truth of immortality to him; many people have. Russell, on the other hand, made a decision early in life to place his trust in the formulations of science, and that trust had worked well enough for him to continue to make that choice. But both men understood that they were believers; they were just believers in different theories of what comes after death. They both chose to believe because they understood that believing is important and can have important consequences in the way we live our lives. It is good to know what you believe and to consider those consequences.

Before we get into some of the possible theories of what happens after death, let's consider what "belief" is. In the end, there are only a few things that we can prove, and while they may be important (2 + 2 = 4, water is made up of hydrogen and oxygen, babies are born from the union of egg and sperm), the good things in life mostly involve belief. We believe that democracy is the most appropriate government, that people are basically good, that service gives life meaning, that the soul survives the body—or we don't believe those things and believe other things. Even the naturalistic belief that we can rely on the information from our senses to give us accurate information is a belief. It is noble and reasonable to believe that there is no such thing as a soul and that this life is completely a matter of molecules and electrons, but that is still a belief. Belief in reincarnation is also noble.

While some people base their beliefs about an afterlife on their own experiences, such as having sensed the presence of a loved one after their death, these experiences cannot be studied, much less proven, by science. These experiences don't come only to those who hope for them and might therefore be indulging in wishful thinking. They come to people who don't believe they are possible and are then faced with a real and often painful dilemma. Do they change their beliefs to incorporate this often quite vivid experience, or dismiss their experience and hang on to old beliefs? Spiritual experiences such as this often fade quickly from our memories; it is almost as if we don't have a mechanism in our brain for remembering them. What then? And how do those of us who have never had such an experience assess the testimony about these experiences from people we trust? Keeping an open mind is an important spiritual task, for, as Ralph Waldo Emerson said, "Nothing is at last sacred but the integrity of one's own mind." (His use of the word *mind* is holistic and includes intuition or, as we might say, mind and heart.) Figuring out what to believe is a great challenge.

There are many theologies concerning what happens after death, and all have their pros and cons. Whether we come to our beliefs about what happens after death by accepting what those around us believe, by exploring many ideas and coming to our own beliefs, or by consulting our personal experiences, our beliefs have consequences, both pros and cons. Below are some potential consequences of several kinds of afterlife beliefs.

Naturalism. The strictly naturalistic approach to life and death is the belief that human beings live and die as plants and animals do. When our bodies die, everything that we are dies. Therefore, our sense of immortality comes from our children, our work, our feeling of connectedness to nature, and the contributions we make to our community and the lives of our loved ones. The advantage of the naturalistic, "this life is it" belief is that it makes our time on earth precious and significant. It is no accident that so many social reforms have come from people who didn't believe in or downplayed afterlife. To them we owe modern hospitals, public schools, social work, humane treatment of the mentally ill, and more. If this life is all there is, it is not precious only to us, it is precious to all human beings.

The disadvantage of Naturalism is that we are tempted to place far more weight on the meaning-making ability of our work and families than these two things can bear. The proverbial stockbrokers who jumped out of windows when Wall Street crashed, the student whose project is rejected, the social worker whose client is unappreciative, or the homemaker whose family resents her doing so much for them are all examples of what happens when we bank too much on our work. Children whose parents need them too much crash in even more tragic ways. They simply can't take the weight of being someone else's immortality. Every kind of afterlife belief has its dangers; this is the danger of Naturalism. Those of us who believe that "this is it" have to practice taking ourselves lightly.

Spirit survival. Many people believe in an afterlife for the spirit, either in the form of reincarnation (the essence of the person survives one human body and goes on to inhabit another human or animal body), or in the form of the spirit at death joining the divine spirit or the Oversoul. These beliefs have the benefit of giving us some connections beyond death. They explain common phenomena such as near-death experiences, some kinds of psychic phenomena, the often observed fact that some people just seem wiser than their experiences can possibly explain, and so on.

However, beliefs about a life after this one have their dangers as well. The most subtle is that they commit us to a dualistic view of human beings—that a human being is made up of a body and a soul that are connected during this life and become disconnected at death. The problem with dualism is that the soul is seen as the more important thing, the body just a vessel—less important, a hindrance to the soul, perhaps even vaguely evil. This belief can have important consequences in society, especially for women, who are in many cultures viewed as more tied up in their bodies than men. In its most extreme and pathological forms, dualism can lead to such tragedies as mass suicide of cult followers who believe that they are throwing off their hindering bodies to free their souls.

It is hard to develop a view of reincarnation which does not reinforce a hierarchical view of human beings or a caste system. The most common understanding of reincarnation goes something like this: If you are a good peasant, you come back as a shopkeeper; if you are a thieving, violent peasant, you come back in a lower form, perhaps as an outcast or an animal. The effect of this theory on social justice and social compassion is dire, since everyone is seen as deserving their lot, whether wealth or misery.

Resurrection. Christianity teaches a very elaborate theory of life after death called Resurrection. It maintains that a human being is a body and soul which are inextricably linked. Christians believe that immortality is not something that just happens to the soul but also happens to the body. It is not a natural occurrence but an intervention by God, who grants an afterlife. Most Christians believe that only some, correctly believing people are resurrected. This teaching has the virtue of skirting some of the problems of dualism, but it is so complex that most Christians do not understand it. As a further downside, it divides human beings into the saved and the damned, which carries unfortunate consequences for human relationships.

Most people feel impelled to adopt some belief about what happens after death. The important thing is to understand the consequences and implications of our beliefs. We must also be aware that our interior and exterior experiences can suggest changes in our beliefs. and as hard as those times of change can be, our integrity requires us to wrestle with them and choose, over and over again, what we believe.

Activities

1. Jot down a few notes; write a poem; or draw a picture, diagram, or symbol of your beliefs about what happens after you die.

2. If you have had an experience of contact with a deceased person, a near-death experience, or another experience that affected your beliefs about what happens after death, write about it.

3. Make a timeline of your life and the various beliefs you have held about life after death at different times. What were you taught as a child? When did you begin to question that? What did you believe as a teen? What did you believe after your first experience of a death? Have you experienced a life-threatening illness or accident?

Questions to Ponder

1. What do you think happens when you die? What experience was formative for you in creating this belief?

2. How do your beliefs about what happens after death affect the way you live your life?

3. What do you hope to leave for future generations? How will that happen?

4. What feelings do you have about what comes after death? Fear? Hope? Certainty? Anticipation?

Think about an experience that was formative for you in creating the belief you now have. Consider what you are willing to share with the group and how to express this.

∾

GATHERING

Candle Lighting

East: Brother Fire, we invoke warmth. May our hearts be open to each other.

South: Father Air, we invoke inspiration. May our words be wise and kind.

West: Sister Water, we invoke the flow of life. May we have courage.

North: Mother Earth, we invoke groundedness. May we all be here in spirit as well as in body.

Leader: Spirit within, we invoke depth. May we remember all we value.

On Our Hearts   10 minutes

Silence   3 minutes

Shared Readings

All men should strive to learn before they die
What they are running from, and to, and why.
  —James Thurber

Alas for those that never sing
But die with all their music in them!
  —Oliver Wendell Holmes

I tend to think of death as being like changing your clothes when
they are old and worn out, rather than as some final end.
  —The Dalai Lama

In the Buddhist approach, life and death are seen as one whole,
where death is the beginning of another chapter of life. Death is a
mirror in which the entire meaning of life is reflected.
  —Sogyal Rinpoche

Death happens. After life's ups and downs, its discoveries and mys-
teries, its smells, and sounds, and colors . . . it ends. And we know
that it will. We know that we will die; that is part of our journey.
And like any journey, we have the choice of planning for it or not.
Rejoicing in it or not. Fearing it or not. After the wondrous surprise of having been born, we are often surprised again when it
comes time to die. Though family and friends, mentors, and even
spiritual guides may have died before us, none have been able to
tell us of their experiences, of what to expect. Though we may be
surrounded by loved ones when it comes time, this journey is ours
alone.
  —Shirley Coe

Sharing   60 minutes

Closing Activity

Closing Words

In the garden the door is always open into the holy—growth, birth, death. Every flower holds the whole mystery in its short cycle, and in the garden we are never far away from death, the fertilizing, good, creative death.

—May Sarton

Song

Announcements

Extinguishing the Candle

East: Brother Fire, thank you for warming our hearts.

South: Father Air, we thank you for inspiring us here.

West: Sister Water, thank you for the courage to be present to the flow of life.

North: Mother Earth, we thank you for grounding us here.

Leader: Spirit within, we take you with us to cherish until we meet again.

Play

∾

BEFORE YOU GATHER

The balance of family and social recreation is becoming harder and harder to come by. The balance of work and real play, activities done for no purpose at all except the release and recapture of energy, is becoming foreign. As a consequence our souls are drying up in work and our minds are being numbed by TV nothingness. We need to learn to play again if our spiritual lives are going to be healthy at all.

—Joan Chittister

Pausing to listen to an airplane in the sky, stooping to watch a ladybug on a plant, sitting on a rock to watch the waves crash over the quayside—children have their own agendas and timescales. As they find out more about their world and their place in it, they work hard not to let adults hurry them. We need to hear their voices.

—Cathy Nutbrown

There often seems to be a playfulness to wise people, as if either their equanimity has as its source this playfulness or the playfulness flows from the equanimity; and they can persuade other people who are in a state of agitation to calm down and manage a smile.

—Edward Hoagland

Consider This

Play. Kids do it—you can hardly stop them! Even children in concentration camps played, in the midst of terror and deprivation. Children's urge to play is so strong because it is their major way of learning. Play helps them master skills, solve problems, learn to exercise their minds, socialize. Even very rough play, the kind that ends in broken bones, black eyes, and hurt feelings, has many uses: Children learn the limits of their prowess, what it feels like to be hurt, and how to repair relationships gone bad. Everyone agrees that play is important for very young children, and there are some researchers who maintain that what happens between school-aged children on the playground is just as important to learning as what happens in the classroom.

Animals play. Many animals play as juveniles, and some—dogs, bears, primates, and ocean mammals, in particular—continue to play as adults. They mock fight, chase each other, and wrestle. They, too, are learning or keeping up skills of survival and socialization. Their antics make us smile. When we go to the zoo, we appreciate the beauty and intricacy of the reptiles and birds. But we hang over the rails watching the sea lions and monkeys. Reptiles and birds are interesting, but they are always dead serious. The organ of play is the big brain.

If you define play as apparently superfluous activity done for its own sake, adults also play, although they are often too serious to call it play. They play sports, play at hobbies, make music, master games, enjoy nature, have sex with no intent to reproduce, and enjoy rambling conversations with friends. Adults play, but most of us don't play as much as we probably should. Modern lifestyles are short on leisure time, and we spend too much of our leisure time in activities like watching TV and surfing the web, which are a little too passive to qualify as play.

There's good reason to be concerned with our lack of active play time. Unlike some animals, such as wolves, which play as juveniles but become dead serious as adults, human adults keep their ability to play. In part, this is surely to ensure that we have some empathy for and ability to stimulate our offspring (and grandchildren) during their long childhoods. But in part it is for our own development. Humans are among only a few animals that are able to make new brain cells and train them in adulthood. We need play in our lives for the same reason children do: to hone new skills, develop new empathies, involve us with new people, teach us our limits, and outfit us for our continuously changing environment. The ability to be playful is an adult trait that helps us solve problems and gives us flexibility. There's a reason for the sayings "dead serious" and "get a life!" We need our play.

Play-deprived people are rigid in their responses to life and have fewer choices than their intelligence would suggest. They tend to approach group tasks as a contest that requires domination or a winner, and they must either be that winner or withdraw if they think they won't be the winner. Those whose life is rich with activities done simply for pleasure and skill-building are much more able to keep that attitude in work and task situations, and are therefore much more fun to work with.

Many parents say that an unexpected joy of parenthood is a second chance to play. Grandparenthood is a third chance, and occupations with children often involve, even necessitate, play. The pediatric nurse who can't be playful is not in the right specialty. Even sick children need to play so they can cope with their circumstances and continue their driving need to develop their skills.

Adults who are not around children much need to work at our play life, because we, too, are still growing and still need to practice our skills, learn our limits, and remind ourselves where we can find our lightness of being. We don't just play to be more effective human beings. We play because its fun!

We often have to rediscover play. If we have children in our lives, they can be our experts. Finding ways to play with them that are fun for us can remind us of the uses of play in our lives. It also models for them that play is an adult activity, too. One teen, speaking to his church at a youth service, thanked the adults in his

Dungeons and Dragons group for showing him that growing up did not require unrelenting seriousness and the end of his imagination. This, he said, gave him hope for his future.

We can set about remembering the play of our own childhoods. What gave us joy then? Did we love playing sports? There are adult teams in every locality. Did we lose ourselves in art or music, stamp collecting or fantasy games? Once again, there are adult versions of these activities available everywhere. Perhaps there were things you always wanted to do but never could, such as surfing, clowning, model trains. Remembering that even the most play-deprived children did play, what did you do and how could you do it as an adult?

Another time in our lives when play is important is courtship. There's a reason that courting couples often dance, play together on sports teams, hike, and build snowmen together. There's no better way to get to know someone than to find out if, and how, they play, and the compatibility of a couple's play life is just as important as their agreements on finances, children, and housing. It often happens that one person introduces their partner to a new kind of play—all the better!

The most direct way to rediscover play is to get our bodies moving. This takes us back to our first play as babies. Dance, exercise, a new sport or physical activity remind us deeply of childhood joy in movement. An indirect way to get ourselves to play is to consider our shadow. What are the less-developed parts of ourselves? What were we told we just couldn't or shouldn't do? Refined boys don't wrestle? Good girls don't get dirty? Our family doesn't bowl, or read, or sing? We don't have to take that as a lifelong prescription. What could be more enriching than doing these things?

Adult play often includes things that children would consider tedious, like sightseeing, opera, reading for pleasure, and hiking. In the adult world, play includes anything done for the sheer joy of it, rather than for a purpose. Naturally, adult joys are larger than children's. There are plenty of things that can be done either playfully or seriously. A yoga class is play for a person who does it because it feels good, while it is a chore for people who do it because the doctor ordered them to slow down. Weaving is play for one person, while another is so obsessed with getting everything perfect that there's nothing playful about it. We can ruin almost any kind of play with too much serious intent; most of us remember that kind of adult interference with our play as children.

Play takes on new importance after retirement. Now, we realize, we do have the time to do the things we were putting off. And we come to see that we don't have all the time in the world to do them in. Retirement communities and senior centers have bridge clubs, dance lessons, and art projects. Senior play is important for quality of life, socializing, staying sharp, and keeping fit. In senior groups, adults often feel less self-conscious about their no-longer-youthful figures, old-fashioned tastes in music, and slower learning curves. And it is still important to play.

Conversation is a form of play, and the sharing of our personal lives that is the point of these Soul to Soul gatherings can also be seen as purposeless, but enriching to our lives. Are you enjoying these gatherings? Are you letting yourself try a variety of the activities offered? That's play!

Activities

1. List some ideas for play that you might like to try. Include activities you do now but would like to spend more time doing. What would it take (time? teammates? new purchases?) to actually give yourself the gift of play? Bring to the gathering an item that symbolizes or is used in one of these kinds of play.

2. Consider how you could arrange to enjoy playtime with children. While their needs and desires have to take precedence, you'll benefit, too. There are many ways to be helpful to kids: teaching religious education, being a big brother or sister, offering to take the children of friends who trust you on outings, and assisting with community activities.

Questions to Ponder

1. What were your favorite activities in childhood?

2. If you quit playing, what did you replace it with?

3. What relationship does play have to your spiritual/religious life? How does play nurture your soul?

4. How is the balance of play in your life? What activities are play in your life now?

5. If you could find more time to just play, what would you fill it with?

Review Activity 1. Also think about a favorite kind of play you experienced as a child that you are willing to share. What was the best part of this playtime?

∽

GATHERING

Candle Lighting

East: Brother Fire, we invoke warmth. May our hearts be open to each other.

South: Father Air, we invoke inspiration. May our words be wise and kind.

West: Sister Water, we invoke the flow of life. May we have courage.

North: Mother Earth, we invoke groundedness. May we all be here in spirit as well as in body.

Leader: Spirit within, we invoke depth. May we remember all we value.

On Our Hearts   10 minutes

Guided Meditation   3 minutes

Shared Readings

Nobody can be uncheered with a balloon.
   —A. A. Milne

My own prescription for health is less paperwork and more running barefoot through the grass.
   —Leslie Grimutter

A child who doesn't play is not a child, but the man who doesn't play has lost forever the child who lived in him and he will certainly miss him.
   —Pablo Neruda

I cannot believe that the inscrutable universe turns on an axis of suffering; surely the strange beauty of the world must somewhere rest on pure joy!
   —Louise Bogan

You can discover more about a person in an hour of play than in a year of conversation.
   —Plato

Sharing   60 minutes

Closing Activity

Closing Words

Playfulness is as sacred as any prayer, or maybe more sacred than any prayer, because playfulness, laughter, singing, dancing will relax you. And the truth is only possible in a relaxed state of being.

—Osho (Bhagwan Shree Rajneesh)

Song

Announcements

Extinguishing the Candle

East: Brother Fire, thank you for warming our hearts.

South: Father Air, we thank you for inspiring us here.

West: Sister Water, thank you for the courage to be present to the flow of life.

North: Mother Earth, we thank you for grounding us here.

Leader: Spirit within, we take you with us to cherish until we meet again.

Prayer

∾

BEFORE YOU GATHER

God listens not to your words save when He Himself utters them through your lips.
—Kahlil Gibran

At a certain point you say to the woods, to the sea, to the mountains, the world, Now I am ready. Now I will stop and be wholly attentive. You empty yourself and wait, listening. After a time you hear it: There is nothing there. There is nothing but those things only, those created objects, discrete, growing or holding, or swaying, being rained on or raining, held, flooding or ebbing, standing, or spread. You feel the world's word as a tension, a hum, a single chorused note everywhere the same. This is it: This hum is the silence.
—Annie Dillard

The best prayers have often more groans than words.
—John Bunyan

If you want the truth, I'll tell you the truth:
Listen to the secret sound, the real sound, which is inside you.
—Kabir

Prayer can be a kind of meditation, a time when you and I open our hearts, open our awareness. Prayer can be a time to reaffirm our concern for other people. Prayer can be a time when we connect with what we hold sacred, a time when we remind ourselves of what is truly important, what really matters to us. Prayer can be a time when we remind ourselves of our highest aspirations and a time when we confront, in all humility and honesty, how we have fallen short of what we strive to be. Prayer can be a time when we quietly rededicate ourselves to becoming what we hope to be. Prayer can be a time for opening ourselves to new possibility, to new direction—a time for listening to that quiet, gentle, persistent voice that dwells in us. We have to be quiet to hear that voice; we have to be still.

—Peter Morales

Consider This

An immigrant from Russia told his grandchildren a story about his father's life in the Old Country. One winter's day, his father was driving home with his horse and sleigh, and a terrible blizzard began. Soon, the man could no longer see through the storm. He was lost and afraid. The wolves howled. It looked like he might not make it home. He thought he might die.

In his fear, the man began to pray. He heard nothing but the howling wind, and he gave in to this terrible situation. He dropped the reins and prepared to die. The horse took off. The wolves seemed very close but the horse went on. Eventually, the man realized that the looming shapes ahead were his house and barn. He leaped out of the sleigh, led the horse into the barn, ran to his own house and fell to his knees in a prayer of thanksgiving to God for his deliverance.

As his descendants heaved a sigh of relief in the warmth and comfort of their New World home, one teenaged cousin whispered to another, "He should have thanked the horse."

This story is funny because it contrasts the relieved true believer with the down-to-earth pragmatist, but a more sophisticated look at the subject of prayer shows us that these two perspectives may not be so far apart. If we think of prayer as our attempt to connect with something larger than our conscious selves, then thanking God for deliverance and thanking the horse for his instinct and strength are not very different.

At a deeper level, the story suggests that prayer might work not only because a true believer asks for something and an all-powerful God grants it, but because prayer gives us access to our own deeper wisdom (which some name God). Perhaps a traditional God guided the horse home. Perhaps, when the frightened man prayed, he relaxed enough that some part of his mind remembered that horses have a very strong homing sense, even in a storm.

To refuse to consider a possibly helpful concept because it is not scientific is to take an unnecessarily literalist approach to life. After all, most adults enjoy the Santa myth and talk about it with the children in their lives. That myth helps us put words and story to the joy of giving and the excitement of waiting. It doesn't have to be true to be useful.

Prayer is similar, an activity that has considerable value and satisfaction, however it works.

There are many kinds of prayer, and asking is only one kind. Prayers of gratitude, prayers which express our pain or bewilderment, and prayers of silence and listening are time-honored in the world's religious traditions. The most expansive definition of prayer is any activity or words which connect a person to God or their higher self, or their highest values.

There are many ways to practice prayer. While some people have a mental picture of prayer as involving kneeling, clasped hands, closed eyes, and lips forming words that are said silently or aloud, there are lots of other kinds of praying, and most people can find a style that works for them. You can pray with chant or song, with exercise such as walking or yoga, and by journaling. One young mother in a Soul to Soul group commented, "I always felt that I was praying as I rocked my baby to sleep; praying for him and his well-being on my good days, and praying for the strength to be a good parent on the bad ones."

You can pray while knitting, doing the dishes, sanding wood, or doing other "mindless" work. If, as you work, you hold in your heart the recipient of the knitting, the people who enjoyed the meal, or your own gratitude, you're praying.

Mother Teresa once said, "Prayer does not demand that we interrupt our work, but that we continue working as if it were a prayer." You can pray using beads, while taking a walk, by counting your breaths, or by looking through an album of pictures of those for whom you pray. Many people pray by lighting candles, not only in church but on the dinner table or a personal altar.

In extreme situations, almost everyone finds themselves praying. "Please may the test results come out okay," we pray, sometimes to our surprise, while waiting for the doctor's call. We know that the words are already printed on the paper, and we don't expect our prayer to change anything, but we pray anyway. "Oh, God, oh, God," we cry, knuckles in our mouth, when something terrible is happening. Whatever our theology, the situation tears it out of us, and this is not a bad thing. Prayer gets us through hard times, sometimes by connecting us to others, sometimes by connecting us to our own wisdom, sometimes by opening us to a peace which may be divine or psychological or both. We don't have to suspend the laws of science to voice our hopes for the future or our empathy for others or our hopes for ourselves. It's valuable to voice them, whatever they are. This wisdom is summed up in the saying, "Birds sing, not because they have an answer. Birds sing because they have a song."

You don't have to believe in any prayer-answering god at all to benefit from speaking or writing out your problems or your pain. The experience of putting your thoughts in order is beneficial in itself. Even if nobody hears, you hear and become your own good listener. Helping professionals will tell you that much of their helpfulness is just that they listen, which allows people to talk and hear themselves and notice their own wisdom as it wells up from within them. Even if you don't want to call this activity prayer, it's good to know that it is identical to the activity that other people call prayer.

Most who believe in a God who answers prayers are aware that this is not magic, with a guaranteed outcome if the "right" person does it "correctly." That's not what they expect from prayer. They get a sense of comfort and possibility from praying, and often the strength to let go of the outcome entirely. "I think it's a coincidence when I get the things I've asked for in prayer," says Brian Taylor, an Episcopal priest and author of several books on the spiritual life. "But I do notice that coincidences seem to happen more often when I pray."

And what if those coincidences happen more often because of the power of human intention, that is, when I have heard myself pray about something I really want, a part of me goes on alert for how to get it? First, that's a good reason to pray. Second, that might be exactly the way God answers prayer. Third, while we will never know, it seems that prayer is a good and useful practice to cultivate.

The activity that some people call meditation and others call praying with silence is beneficial for mind, body, and spirit. When we give ourselves permission to be quiet, to pay no attention to our eternally chattering "monkey mind," to just rest in the moment, our blood pressure goes down and all kinds of other beneficial things happen to our body. We get a mental rest from the rigors of planning, worrying, and thinking. And sometimes in the space we make, we hear the still, small voice of our inner knowledge, the collective unconscious, or God.

This kind of prayer does not involve stopping thinking. The mind thinks by nature. We are more likely to cultivate an inner silence by working at not paying attention to the mind's chatter, just as we don't pay attention to, say, the diners around us in a crowded restaurant.

Praying for others is also a powerful practice, whether with words or by gazing at their picture, sending energy, or holding their faces in our mind's eye. Even skeptics are usually touched when told that someone is praying for them, and people who feel loved and connected to others seem to have better outcomes from difficult times than those who feel isolated.

For many of us, the hardest prayer of all is praying for people with whom we feel angry or distant, or for someone who is persecuting us in some way. Many who have struggled with this, however, have found that when they can pray for or wish their enemy peace and well-being, the prayer often transforms the situation and brings peace and a sense of well-being to the one who is praying. This is a perfect example of the powerful remark by Lon Ray Call, "Prayer doesn't change things. Prayer changes people, and people change things."

Even without getting answers, you can find the practice of prayer satisfying and helpful, well worth the time spent experimenting to find practices that work. By allowing yourself to loosen your grip on magical expectations and rigid definitions of prayer, your life can be richer, wiser, and more peaceful, and you can connect to the world's religious people and their nearly universal practices of prayer.

Activities

1. Try a couple of these ways to pray:

   Following your breath. Breathe in a normal rhythm using a phrase like "Peace in" on the in-breath and "Peace out" on the out-breath. Start with two minutes and increase the time as you get more comfortable.

   Being still. Sit with a still mind for just a little longer than is comfortable. As thoughts enter your mind, let them go by as ships passing by on a river. Don't follow the thoughts, just let them float by.

   Prayer beads. String together three or four beads that symbolize people in your life. Each night before bed, touch the beads, bringing these people to your mind in a loving way. You may want to have the beads symbolize yourself, people you love, people you have conflict with, and finally the whole world. You may purchase or make a string of prayer beads and use them to time a breathing meditation.

Walking prayer. Try walking barefoot (traditional, but optional if not practical) slowly for five minutes with no destination in mind. With each mindful step imagine you are caressing the earth or floor with your foot.

Walking a labyrinth. Try "walking" this finger labyrinth. Before you begin, focus on a question, issue, person, or hope. Slowly trace the path with your finger until you get to the center. Rest for a few minutes, then journey back out again. Lauren Artress, author and Episcopal priest, says this about walking a labyrinth, "Most of us carry questions subliminally. . . . Part of the preparation for your labyrinth walk can be to bring these questions into your conscious mind. . . . There is nothing magical about the labyrinth. It simply allows our consciousness to open so that deeper, and perhaps new, parts of ourselves can speak to us more directly." If you want to really walk a labyrinth you can probably find one in a park or at a church in your area. You may locate one on the Internet.

Visualization. Read through these directions several times before following them. Sit quietly in a chair with your eyes closed, breathing normally. Imagine light coming in through the top of your head and slowly moving down though your body until each part of you has been filled with light. Then visualize the light moving out from your heart area and encircling those you love.

A prayer candle. Put a candle in your home, perhaps on the kitchen table or on a shelf in the living room. Light the candle while thinking of someone who is "on your heart."

Listening to music. Sit in a comfortable position and listen to soothing calm music. Brian Eno's *Music for Airports,* Carlos Nakai's *Canyon Trilogy,* or *Journey of the Cosmos* by Brainwave-Sync are good choices.

Lectio Divina (Sacred Reading). Read a passage slowly, ponder it, notice what word or phrase jumps out at you, be still for a few minutes, and see what comes to you. Try it with the Psalm below or with a favorite poem.

2. Read the following prayer, which is adapted from a psalm, and then write your own adaptation of this psalm. Make it your own prayer.

> Great Mother, hear my prayer,
> the love, the longings of my heart.
> Hold my life, be with me in the night,
> melt me down to my essence.
> Help me live in love and justice. Guide me—
> Teach me your love.
> Shield me from those who would hurt me.
> Help me to leave this world a better place
> And see your face in it all.
> —Psalm 17, adapted by Christine Robinson

Questions to Ponder

1. Try to remember some childhood experiences with prayer. Did anybody teach you to pray when you were a child? Did you ever try it? Did someone pray with you or require you to pray?

2. What is the role of silence in your spiritual life?

3. When have you been an answer to someone's prayer?

4. What prayer form described in the activities above holds an interest for you?

5. What is your definition of prayer?

Think about an experience of prayer in your childhood you are willing to share with the group. Think about one of the many forms of prayer that resonates with you. Consider how you will share this.

∽

GATHERING

Candle Lighting

East: Brother Fire, we invoke warmth. May our hearts be open to each other.

South: Father Air, we invoke inspiration. May our words be wise and kind.

West: Sister Water, we invoke the flow of life. May we have courage.

North: Mother Earth, we invoke groundedness. May we all be here in spirit as well as in body.

Leader: Spirit within, we invoke depth. May we remember all we
value.

On Our Hearts 10 minutes

Metta or Loving Kindness Meditation 5 minutes

Shared Readings

Some of my best prayers have been arguments with God.
  —as told to Gail Godwin

Ultimately the person who really needs to hear my prayer is me.
The person who needs to hear your prayer is you. The people who
need to heed our collective prayer is us.
  —Peter Morales

O Mother Earth from whom we receive our food. . . . Every step
that we take upon You should be done in a sacred manner; each
step should be as a prayer.
  —Black Elk

In prayer, we are likely . . . to see ourselves as we really are. We can't
expect that we are going to be healed of the deep wounds of our
heart without seeing what those wounds are.
  —Roberta Bondi

Even emptiness itself is prayer, if we can permit ourselves to understand emptiness as part of the rhythm of the breath of God.
  —Nancy Roth

What I'd really like is for my life to be a prayer, an offering of
thanksgiving. I could do it if I were always present, but I'm not.
  —Sylvia Boorstein

Sharing   60 minutes

Closing Activity

Closing Words

Go now in peace.
Deeply regard each other.
Truly listen to each other.
Speak what each of you must speak.
Be ready in any moment to disarm your own heart,
and always live as if a realm of love had begun.
So be it. Blessed be. Amen.
    —Barbara Hamilton-Holway

Song

Announcements

Extinguishing the Candle

East: Brother Fire, thank you for warming our hearts.
South: Father Air, we thank you for inspiring us here.
West: Sister Water, thank you for the courage to be present to
           the flow of life.
North: Mother Earth, we thank you for grounding us here.
Leader: Spirit within, we take you with us to cherish until we
           meet again.

Resilience

∽

BEFORE YOU GATHER

Resilience is a nuanced and fluid concept, being more of a process that leads to relatively positive outcomes over time rather than a fixed trait of the individual adult or child.
—Dorothy Scott and Fiona Arney

According to Darwin's *Origin of Species*, it is not the most intellectual of the species that survives; it is not the strongest that survives; but the species that survives is the one that is able best to adapt and adjust to the changing environment in which it finds itself.
—Leon C. Megginson

In the middle of winter I at last discovered that there was in me an invincible summer.
—Albert Camus

Go within every day and find the inner strength so that the world will not blow your candle out.
—Katherine Dunham

You're braver than you believe, and stronger than you seem, and smarter than you think.
—*Pooh's Great Adventure*

Consider This

Ten adults are laid off, or experience messy divorces, make serious mistakes, have serious health problems, become involved in disasters, or lose people they love—all the stuff of life that launches us into unwelcome, uncomfortable, inevitable change. Four of those adults sail through, seemingly without much distress, and remake their lives. Five endure a period of misery and difficulty, then find their balance and their energy on some new life path, learn, grow, and recover with new insights. One takes longer and needs more help, but even that person is very likely to eventually recover.

The differences amongst these ten probably don't have much to do with how disruptive the change, how devastating the mistake, how serious the illness, or how painful the loss. The differences between those who thrive and those who struggle have more to do with a skill set and maturity level called resilience.

"Stress-hardiness" is how one researcher defines resilience, and since all of us have experienced stress in our lives and survived that stress, we all have at least some resilience. Our lives are a succession of changes, both incremental and disruptive, happy and wretched, and we have to cope, learn, adapt, and let go over and over. Nor do those changes come politely, at the predictable and manageable rate of one per year. Instead, they seem to pile up on each other suddenly after a stretch of tranquility. Since you are reading this, you are a monument to the human ability to cope with change, tragedy, social ills, crisis, growth, aging, happiness, grief, turns of fortune, and a host of other challenges.

But you may not feel resilient enough. You may not feel able to cope with aging and family changes *and* an uncertain economy all at once, for instance. Or you may not feel resilient enough to cope with the demands of changing jobs, year after year. Or you may wonder if you are resilient enough to go to memorial service after memorial service as friends and loved ones die. You may be aware of how much you have weathered but feel depleted as you face the future.

You can take heart in knowing that the human animal was engineered by evolution to deal with stress. Although Sigmund Freud started us thinking that dealing with stressful events was difficult and upsetting, and that we probably require help to do it well, his theories about this have been debunked over the years. Most people, even those who endure extremely stressful losses or disasters, bounce back in a fairly short time, and most of the rest bounce back in a somewhat longer time. There is no one-size-fits-all prescription for that bouncing back; we all do it in our own unique time and way. Some people need to talk about it, some don't. Some will become quite dependent for a short period and need the care of others. Most soldier on. Some will be extremely emotional and others will feel numb. There is no one way to be resilient, and sometimes we have to tell those around us, "I have to do this my own way." We'll want to reassess our way after some time has passed and be open to another tactic if we're not doing and feeling better.

We know some things about resilience, and they start with what we know about stress. Simply put, when we feel threatened, our bodies go on high alert, preparing us for fight or flight. Blood rushes to our large muscles, hormones pour into our system to strengthen us, our vision is narrowed, our hearing dims, our fine motor coordination nearly disappears. Our ancestors didn't need to dial phones when the saber-toothed tiger attacked; they needed to run! Once the threat is over, the blood supply returns to normal and the body begins to detoxify all the chemicals which caused this reaction. We feel cold because our core has cooled down with blood supply elsewhere, and we may feel shaky from the stress hormones, but we quickly return to normal.

And a good thing, too, because while those stress-management chemicals may save our lives by pumping us up to fight or flee, over the long term they are not good for our bodies. A person who is constantly threatened or always in a fight-or-flight state of high arousal can suffer long-term health consequences. Therefore, our bodies have several mechanisms for returning to normal after a threat has passed. Some people have better mechanisms than others; this is a genetic inheritance and there's not much we can do about it.

However, there is plenty we can do to enhance our natural resilience. We can start these practices any time, but it is best if we start them before we need them. They are not tips for managing stress during times of change but are basic life practices, chosen and practiced regularly, which build resilience for hard times. As a bonus, they also enhance our experience of life in stable times as well as disruptive ones.

Our spirituality is a major component of our stress-hardiness. Whether you see yourself as a child of God or as a part of the human race with each member having worth and dignity, whether you think your great purpose is growing in love and service or raising a child or adding to the store of human knowledge, your beliefs and living according to those beliefs are important to your resilience. Worship, meditation, prayer, and reflection give us practice in valuing our strivings while recognizing that our ultimate values are not at risk. This may be, most of all, what keeps us recovering from all the little blows and outrages to our hopes and intentions which life brings. In addition, we know that meditative practices help the body recover from its stress responses.

Crisis and change are hard work. If we are in the habit of eating properly and exercising, we will be better able to deal with whatever comes our way. It's likely that good nutrition builds up our ability to deal with stress, and there is no doubt that exercise helps us to regulate stress hormones. Good networks of family, friendship, and community support are nice to have in good times and absolutely essential in difficult times. The people around us can shelter us when shock or grief has left us vulnerable. They can remind us that we are not the only person to go through such a trial. They can keep us in touch with our strengths when we've been knocked off of our pins. Their care reminds us at a basic level of the care we got as children, which kicks in our sense of basic trust that one way or another things will be okay. We all know these things, and we re-learn how important they are with every crisis in our lives. It is easy to get too busy to do the work of exercising, eating properly, and building networks, yet often people say, when they get to the other side of a crisis, that the silver lining in that cloud was that they were reminded of the importance of their support systems.

There are a few habits of mind and heart that, practiced in good times, will add to our resilience. One is investing our energy in our inner self, rather than in appearances and belongings. As long as we live, we have our self and our sense of integrity. Our possessions, job, role, beauty, and even skills can leave us.

One survivor of a Japanese concentration camp and later a psychiatrist, John Nardini, remembered that the POWs who survived those terrible, abusive circumstances were the ones who had a firm sense of self. They could remember who they were even when nothing in their immediate situation confirmed them. "They can treat us like animals, but that doesn't make us animals," someone told him. This firm sense of self is also called having good boundaries. POWs whose sense of self was not so firm tended to melt into the abusive situation and lose heart and health more quickly than those who held to their values, remembered that they were loved, and kept heart through their captivity.

Another part of the skill set of resilience is the ability to ask for help and support. Many of us find that hard to do, and we should find appropriate ways to practice it. Even asking for directions in a strange city is hard for some people. If you are such a person, forcing yourself to do it will not only get you to where you are going faster, it is a little practice session for getting help with bigger things.

There are religious teachings and life philosophies that help us survive adversity. They include the belief or sense that God cares about our suffering and desires a good outcome for us. Another is the Taoist belief that change is the essence of life and going with the flow is the best way to manage things. Humanists will find special solace in our ability to learn and grow from adversity. The person who can say, "I lost my entire inheritance and had to learn

a marketable skill" or "My partner left me and I was forced to realize how selfish I had been, and why," has not only stayed afloat in a
storm but has learned to swim.

All of us, even those who feel presently battered by some storm,
have ridden the waves of life successfully, resiliently. With a little
help from our friends, our faith, and our basic habits of self-care—
living out our values, asking for help when we need it, and tending
to our communities and relationships—we mostly manage to be
resilient enough to ride even the big waves of change, a part of all
that is our life.

Activities

1. Think of yourself as a boat or a bird, floating on a body of
water. What kind of water would represent your life right now?
A fast-moving stream? A stormy ocean? A calm pond? What
kind of boat or bird are you? What kind of shape is your boat
or bird in? Draw a picture or write a paragraph.

2. Look at this checklist of factors that bolster resilience and add
others if you wish. Star the ones that are well expressed in your
life, and jot down the ways in which you express them. Put an
exclamation point by the ones you feel are lacking in your life.
Jot down a few ideas you might try for growing them. Put a
question mark by the ones you're not sure about and want to
explore.

Having a spiritual life
Taking care of yourself physically
Having family/friend/community networks
Investing energy on inner self
Asking for help

3. Make a map of your support network. Put a stick figure with
your name on it in the center of a sheet of paper. Starting with

the people closest to you and moving out from there, write the names of people who are in your networks of caring and support in all areas of your life.

Questions to Ponder

1. Think back on the past few years. What changes have come your way in health, relationships, jobs, etc.? List as many changes as you can and note how you handled them. Were you happy or miserable? Did you cope or are you still reeling from the consequences of the change?

2. To whom do you go for help when you're down and discouraged? Whom have you asked to help you in difficult situations in the past few years?

3. When you are suffering, what brings you relief? A spiritual practice, talking with a friend, looking within yourself? How do you cope with the stresses of life?

4. When have you learned from your mistakes? Are you striving to learn from a mistake now?

5. What area of the factors that bolster resilience are you most in need of growing?

Do Activity 1. Bring your picture or paragraph to share with the group. Think about how you want to share it.

GATHERING

Candle Lighting

East: Brother Fire, we invoke warmth. May our hearts be open to each other.

South: Father Air, we invoke inspiration. May our words be wise and kind.

West: Sister Water, we invoke the flow of life. May we have courage.

North: Mother Earth, we invoke groundedness. May we all be here in spirit as well as in body.

Leader: Spirit within, we invoke depth. May we remember all we value.

On Our Hearts   10 minutes

Silence   3 minutes

Shared Readings

Man never made any material as resilient as the human spirit.
—Bern Williams

You desire to know the art of living, my friend? It is contained in one phrase: Make use of suffering.
—Henri Frédéric Amiel

At the center of your being you have the answer; you know who you are and you know what you want.
—Lao Tzu

Nothing in the world can take the place of persistence. Talent will not; nothing is more common than unsuccessful men with talent. Genius will not; unrewarded genius is almost a proverb. Education will not; the world is full of educated derelicts. Persistence and determination are omnipotent.
—Calvin Coolidge

Your time is limited, so don't waste it living someone else's life. . . . Don't let the noise of others' opinions drown out your own inner voice. And most important, have the courage to follow your heart and intuition.
—Steve Jobs

Sharing 60 minutes

Closing Activity

Closing Words

People are like stained-glass windows. They sparkle and shine when the sun is out, but when the darkness sets in, their true beauty is revealed only if there is a light from within.
—Elisabeth Kübler-Ross

Song

Announcements

Extinguishing the Candle

East: Brother Fire, thank you for warming our hearts.

South: Father Air, we thank you for inspiring us here.

West: Sister Water, thank you for the courage to be present to the flow of life.

North: Mother Earth, we thank you for grounding us here.

Leader: Spirit within, we take you with us to cherish until we meet again.

Aging

∿

BEFORE YOU GATHER

The evening of life brings with it its lamp.
—Joseph Joubert

We are surprised by the youthful vitality and unmarked face when we see earlier photos of ourselves. When we look in the mirror, we reluctantly acknowledge the aging mask. It seems that there is no escaping the marks of life. Every experience that we have, everything that we do and think is registered upon us as surely as the steady embroidery of a tattoo artist. But to a large degree, the pattern and picture that will emerge is up to us.
—Deng Ming-Dao

Old age was growing inside me. It kept catching my eye from the depths of the mirror. I was paralyzed sometimes as I saw it making its way toward me so steadily when nothing inside me was ready for it.
—Simone de Beauvoir

The model that I'm proposing does more than restore the elder to a position of honor and dignity based on age and long life experience. It envisions the elder as an agent of evolution, attracted as much by the future of humanity's expanded brain-mind potential as by the wisdom of the past. With an increased lifespan and the psychotechnologies to expand the mind's frontiers, the spiritual elder heralds the next phase of human and global development.

—Zalman Schachter-Shalomi and Ronald S. Miller

Consider This

Although very few of us look forward to it, aging is one of the great tasks of our lives. It's right up there with learning to love, to forgive, to risk—hard work, but when accomplished, enriching and very satisfying. We take the first steps on this important journey by giving aging its proper place in the life cycle and remembering that all the changes of our lives bring their joys and their difficulties.

The trajectory of childhood is "growing up," something which has a positive ring to adults. Children are often less delighted to hear how they've grown or that "you're becoming a man now." They are more aware than forgetful adults of the losses that attend growing up. That simple and sleek child's body becomes complicated, awkward, and harder to care for, and while children love new privileges, they are naturally less excited about new responsibilities. There's no choice, though. We begin as children moving through the dance of loss and gain that is life.

Once we reach adulthood, our trajectory is no longer "growing up." Tell an adult to "grow up" and you've delivered a major insult. Adults continue their journey into wisdom by "maturing," and while maturing has its losses of young adult figure, vigor, and wild oats, maturing is seen as a mostly positive task, and maturity is something we feel we should attain by midlife. But after that, all the positive gloves are off. When midlife ends at about age sixty, we no longer "grow up" and we no longer "mature"; instead, we "age."

Aging doesn't seem to have the balance of positive and negative that growing and maturing did. Now our reaction is not just mixed. It's profoundly negative. "It's all downhill from here!" we say. And yet, that aging phase of our lives is likely to last between fifteen and thirty years, one-fifth to one-third of our lifespan. It's a tragedy to think of these years as negatively as we do. This time in our lives holds as many opportunities for growth, satisfaction, and meaning, as it does difficulty and loss.

Science suggests that our negativity about the elder years is unfounded. Evolutionary biologists who are focused on the survival of the species ask, "What is the evolutionary purpose of such a long life?" Most animals do not live past their reproductive years, but apparently there is genetic benefit in longevity for humans, and families with long-life genes do better on an evolutionary scale. These scientists believe that the presence of grandparents and other older adults is beneficial to the community as a whole, and especially to children. In other words, long lives mean a surplus of adults in family groups, and that's a good thing.

Although there have always been some people who lived into their seventh, eighth, or even ninth decades, it is a new thing in human society for a large number of people to remain vigorous into their eighties. This generation of elders is inventing new meanings and contributions for this time of life. Rabbi Zalman Schachter-Salomi writes of "aging and saging," and suggests that the aging years are for spiritual and personal development after life's responsibilities have been taken care of. This is also the wisdom of the Hindus, who say that after the householder stage of life comes retirement, which in that culture means not just leaving paid work, but also withdrawing from outward life to enjoy contemplation and growth in peace and wisdom. Joan Chittister, a Benedictine sister, writes that our elder years, like our young adulthood, are a time when we can remake our lives into a new pattern. She encourages using this time for personal and spiritual growth. She says, "We are here to depart from this world as finished as we can possibly become. Old age is not when we stop growing. It is exactly the period in which we set out to make sense out of all the growing we have already done."

The counterculture generation should take note: Aging well by the above definitions is profoundly countercultural. Our culture doesn't want us to turn inward and grow in spirit. We don't consume enough that way. Our culture would much rather we chased youthful bodies with expensive medical treatments and products, make-up and clothing, and forgot our troubles with endless traveling. People who are at peace with themselves, who enjoy their families and friends and face death with clear vision, are not good consumers. It seems likely that the Baby Boomers will redefine aging as they redefined youth and young adulthood.

For most new graduates of middle age, the first task of aging is to find our elder calling. What contributions will we make in our older years? Will we have the luxury of making those contributions without being paid? Senior volunteers, from the Peace Corps to the local church, bring their life's wisdom, energy, and compassion to the places it is most needed. And while many opportunities for service close down as our bodies close down, our service to others continues to our last breath. In Madeleine L'Engle's *A Ring of Endless Light*, Grandfather Austin, a retired Episcopalian priest who is now debilitated and facing death, notes that at this time of his life his vocation is simply to pray for the world. Younger generations watch their elders accept death and are often inspired to greater love and service, and less fear, in their own lives.

Even if we continue to work at our same vocation, we may feel drawn to develop some talent either long ago put away or newly discovered. It often happens that we discover new interests, new ways to play, and new hobbies as we grow older. Post-retirement, we can really loosen up on the personality traits that kept us productive workers and explore something new. And now we have the time for it. The scientist finds himself tutoring children. The economist takes up water colors. The bus driver starts a garden. The teacher starts rehabbing old houses.

Some people find joy in continuing to develop their life's call. They continue in a satisfying profession as consultants, continue to serve institutions they love on boards and as philanthropists. They continue to grow and innovate. The painter John Marin (1870–1953) was hospitalized late in life, and when he came home he experimented with applying paint with medical syringes. That attitude of curiosity and continued growth is the hallmark of a person who is aging but still very much alive.

The second task of aging is an inward one. It is a task of spiritual growth, life review, and coming to terms with our lives. It is not uncommon for people to awaken in spiritual interest as they enter their aging years. Sometimes this is simply because they now have time to scratch an itch that's been around for a while. Sometimes the crisis of retirement sends them to church. While aging will bring a waning of physical energy, our spiritual energy can be strong. And a more leisurely way of life means for some a deepening appreciation of the present moment.

Our aging bodies will require better balance of us, and graceful aging is also a matter of dealing with the decrease in bodily power and the increase in time and effort spent on staying healthy, and coming to terms with illness and death. Many people would like to put their fears and feelings about this out of their minds and pretend that they will go on forever more or less as they are now. But that doesn't work, especially if we don't take proper care of ourselves. Good aging requires us to confront our mortality and our beliefs about what happens after death.

We begin graceful aging quite young, actually—or we begin a life-long habit of denial. When we first realize that we just can't eat as much as we used to without gaining weight, when we start hearing the ticking of our reproductive clocks, when our doctors order new and different tests, when our joints start to get stiff—all these are warm-ups for the rigors of aging. The first friends to die in our generation give us a wake-up call to the rigors of grieving. If we can embrace the tasks and feelings these changes bring, we are well on our way to graceful aging.

Activities

1. Gather five photos of yourself taken over as wide a span of years as possible. What do you notice about your appearance? How do you feel about this?

2. Make a collage using pictures from a magazine that symbolizes how you feel about aging at this point in your life (like a ship sailing, a tree, a person running a race, a frustrated person, a pretty sunset, etc.).

Questions to Ponder

1. When people think about aging, they often have fears about particular parts of the process. Which of the following trouble you the most: physical decline, grieving, mental decline, losing a spouse, feeling useless, requiring care from children or strangers, dying, death?

2. Who have you known who aged well? What qualities does this person have? How do/did your parents handle aging?

3. What signs of aging affect you right now? List some of your losses in the past two years, such as beauty, career, strength, money, loved ones, or mental sharpness.

4. What plans have you put in place to ensure your care in your elder years?

5. Some speak of autumn years as the time when we gather the fruits of our labors. What fruits of your life are you enjoying or do you hope to enjoy in these harvest years?

Think about how you are experiencing loss as part of aging. Be prepared to share some of these age-related losses and how you are handling them.

∾

GATHERING

Candle Lighting

East: Brother Fire, we invoke warmth. May our hearts be open to each other.

South: Father Air, we invoke inspiration. May our words be wise and kind.

West: Sister Water, we invoke the flow of life. May we have courage.

North: Mother Earth, we invoke groundedness. May we all be here in spirit as well as in body.

Leader: Spirit within, we invoke depth. May we remember all we value.

On Our Hearts   10 minutes

Silence   3 minutes

Shared Readings

To know how to grow old is the masterwork of wisdom, and one of the most difficult chapters in the great art of living.
    —Henri Frederic Amiel

I suppose real old age begins when one looks backward rather than forward, but I look forward with joy to the years ahead and especially to the surprises that any day may bring.
    —May Sarton

Each part of life has its own pleasures. Each has its own abundant harvest, to be garnered in season. We may grow old in body, but we need never grow old in mind and spirit.

—Cicero

If we accept and internalize the fact of our own mortality, then by definition, we have to deal with the essential questions of how we live and how we spend our allotted time. We have to stop procrastinating, pretending that we have forever to do what we want to do and be what we long to be.

—Lama Surya Das

A man's age is something impressive, it sums up his life: maturity reached slowly and against many obstacles, illnesses cured, griefs and despairs overcome, and unconscious risks taken; maturity formed through so many desires, hopes, regrets, forgotten things, loves. A man's age represents a fine cargo of experiences and memories.

—Antoine de Saint-Exupéry

Sharing   60 minutes

Closing Activity

Closing Words

Elders come to terms with their mortality, harvest the wisdom of their years, and transmit a legacy to future generations. Serving as mentors, they pass on the distilled essence of their life experience to others. The joy of passing on wisdom to younger people not only seeds the future, but crowns an elder's life with worth and nobility.

—Zalman Schachter-Shalomi and Ronald S. Miller

Song

Announcements

Extinguishing the Candle

East: Brother Fire, thank you for warming our hearts.

South: Father Air, we thank you for inspiring us here.

West: Sister Water, thank you for the courage to be present to the flow of life.

North: Mother Earth, we thank you for grounding us here.

Leader: Spirit within, we take you with us to cherish until we meet again.

Blessings

 ～

BEFORE YOU GATHER

A blessing is not something that one person gives another. A blessing is a moment of meeting, a certain kind of relationship in which both people involved remember and acknowledge their true nature and worth, and strengthen what is whole in one another. . . . Blessing life moves us closer to each other and closer to our authentic selves.
    —Rachel Naomi Remen

When I had breast cancer for the second time, I was jolted into a new realization about the time I have on this earth. I saw my past life through a lens of gratitude, which led to a spiritual practice of thanksgiving and blessing. I want to let everyone know how special they are to me, how much I cherish having them in my life. I choose to let my soul be seen and connect with other souls, for our time together on earth is so fleeting.
    —Alicia Hawkins

Blessing involves relationship: One does not bless without investing something of oneself into the receiver of one's blessing. And one does not receive blessing oblivious of its gracious giver. A blessing spirituality is a relating spirituality. And if it is true that all of creation flows from a single, loving source, then all of creation is blessed and is a blessing.

—Matthew Fox

Consider This

"Bless you!" we say, when somebody sneezes. We might do it reflexively, but the thought behind the action is that sneezing equals illness and the sneezer is in need of our sympathy or prayer. (Actually, the tradition hearkens back to a time when people thought that a sneeze was one moment when a demon could enter a person's body, and that this could be averted by a blessing. But the prayer for health is the same!)

"I'm counting my blessings," we say, when a challenge arises in an otherwise good life and it helps to remind ourselves of all that we have and can count on during this difficult time. One hallmark of spiritual maturity is awareness of our blessings.

These days, more and more people are attending pet blessings (where the importance of our pets and our love for them is held up by a religious community) and house blessings (where the new occupant shares the process of making a house a home with friends and spiritual communities). These and other rituals come to us from the distant past, but they were relatively rare except in certain religious traditions. Now they happen throughout the religious and non-religious spectrum. So do various kinds of blessings of couples who are beginning or continuing a partnership.

These three uses of the concept of blessing are interrelated and seem to be reemerging in the spiritual practices of younger generations. One understanding of a blessing is that it is a little prayer, offered quickly in everyday situations. The sneeze-blessing has made it into common speech, but many spiritually inclined people, especially if they are part of a spiritual culture, are intentional about making many blessings throughout the day. In *Fiddler on the Roof* the new owner of the amazing sewing machine asks the Rabbi if there is a blessing for a sewing machine. The Rabbi says, "Of course; in our religion there is a blessing for everything!" and then proceeds to intone a long sentence in Hebrew that ends with a very English, "sewing machine." Audiences can be counted on to laugh at the juxtaposition of a sacred, ancient tongue with the modern, work-a-day words "sewing machine," but all blessings have a bit of that irony in them, as they bring the sacred world into the secular one for a moment.

In this secular society, prayers are supposed to be private, or at least kept between persons of similar faith, and the most socially correct "bless you" is the perfunctory one, uttered in a way that seems unconscious of its deep meaning. But every once in a while, perhaps after the third sneeze, one hears a "bless you" that seems to be a sincere well-wishing, and we appreciate that. It's a small healing of spirit, if not of lungs, to know that someone cares. "Bless your heart!" is another saying we use when someone tells us of a difficulty in their life and if we say it as if we mean it, it conveys our special sympathy and hope that the hearer will surmount this problem. These little prayers can slip by even our secular filters and can be deeply appreciated by recipients and, perhaps as important, remind the giver of our human vocation to care about each other and be blessings in each others' lives. There are other ways to bless without breaking the secular taboos: A heartfelt "I wish you well," spoken with conviction and eye contact, feels like a blessing, and so does a simple vase of flowers left on a desk with a note that says not only "Get well," but also "Blessings in this time of illness." And among those whom we know will be appreciative of our spiritual perspective, we can take more risks with blessing and being blessed.

A blessing can also refer to any part of our life which is good and which we think of as a gift, which we might have worked for but which we don't imagine that we deserve. When we count our blessings, we deliberately adopt a positive mindset, recalling what we usually take for granted: the people in our lives who care about us, our health, our material wealth, our joy in using our talents, our sense that we are supposed to be doing what we are doing (our vocation or calling), even the gift of life itself. This not only helps our rational mind put our current troubles in perspective, it helps our intuitive mind say, "It's going to be okay, I can handle this"— both sides of the exercise are useful as we move through difficulty.

The spiritual practice of counting our blessings is honored widely in the world's faiths. Gratitude is a reality check: In fact, nothing we could ever accomplish earns us the gift of life. A practice of gratitude reminds us to be humble. The upwelling of gratitude is a very pleasant feeling to most people, and it is ours, whatever our theology. We certainly can thank God for these gifts, if we believe in God. If we don't, the gratitude itself is sufficient.

Finally, a blessing is a ritual, a way of nurturing our good intentions and hopes for the future by acting as if they were actually that way in the present, in a carefully prepared moment. We hold these rituals only for the most important things in our lives: our children, our partnerships, our homes, our pets. Rituals don't have magical properties. A blessed pet may run in front of a car and die the next day, and every blessed partnership, like every unblessed one, ends eventually. That's not to say that blessings have no effect. When we take the time and effort to go to a pet blessing and while there reminded of how much that animal adds to our lives, we are more likely to do everything possible to keep our pet safe. When we go to the time and expense of holding a house blessing and are surrounded by the warmth of good friends who wish us well, our home becomes more homelike. We can relax into the good things that will happen there, and our relationships are all the more solid because of the care we have put into them.

The most common blessing which we all participate in (often unknowingly) is the English "good-bye," which is a contraction of "God be with you," a reminder that we are held in mystery throughout our lives. It's nearly the same in Spanish (*adios*) and French (*adieu*), both of which mean "to God!" "Godspeed" is now out of use, but we know what it means and sometimes call on it when the circumstances are just right. The informal "farewell" is a secular version of this same blessing.

There is something so especially fraught about partings that our language-molding forebears felt the need to give blessings, and we feel a need to keep giving them, even if we are usually unconscious of their full meaning. There is wisdom here. Our significant partings—the parting of spouses for a day's work or the parting of people who have enjoyed each other in a group meeting for the last time—deserve a special good-bye.

"Good-bye" itself means something like "over and out" to most people these days. So if we really want to give people a blessing as we part company, we have to be deliberate about it, perhaps naming a hope for them or a way that our meeting was a blessing to us, and then voicing our hope for their future. "Thanks for taking the time to meet with me," we might say. "You were very helpful. And congratulations on your promotion. You'll be able to do a lot of good in this office. May it be a joy to you!"

That's a blessing!

Activities

1. Look over these various ways to say good-bye. Many of them convey a blessing from God. Which of these have you used? What are other ways you say good-bye?

   Godspeed (Middle English): May God speed you on your journey.
   Farewell (Middle English): May you fare well in the world.
   Auf Wiedersehen (German): Until I see you again.
   Good-bye (English): God be with you.
   Adieu (French): I commend you to God.
   Adios (Spanish): I commend you to God.
   Vaya con dios (Spanish): Go with God.
   Slan abhaile (Irish): Safe homewards.
   Shalom (Hebrew): Peace.
   Namaste (Sanskrit): The divine peace in me greets the divine peace in you.

2. Make a picture of all the blessings in your life. You can draw, cut pictures out of magazines, make a time line, etc. Think of people in your life, things of nature, places you've lived, other things you love.

3. Make a space in your home to keep representations of the blessings in your life. You might include pictures of people you love or places that are important to you, or symbols or keepsakes of key blessings in your life, such as a dried flower from your garden, a favorite quote or two, and a candle. Spend some time gazing at all your blessings.

Questions to Ponder

1. What is a blessing?

2. How has this group been a blessing for you?

3. Who has been a blessing to you throughout your life?

4. What are other blessings in your life? Think of times in nature, places you've been, gifts you have been blessed with, such as a great soprano voice, a love for your job, a healthy body, etc.

5. When and for what reason have you given a blessing?

Be prepared to share some of your blessings with the group. For instance, you might list your children, your dog, loving parents, a fulfilling job. Think about which blessings you are willing to share.

GATHERING

Candle Lighting

East: Brother Fire, we invoke warmth. May our hearts be open to each other.

South: Father Air, we invoke inspiration. May our words be wise and kind.

West: Sister Water, we invoke the flow of life. May we have courage.

North: Mother Earth, we invoke groundedness. May we all be here in spirit as well as in body.

Leader: Spirit within, we invoke depth. May we remember all we value.

On Our Hearts   10 minutes

Silence   3 minutes

Shared Readings

Sometimes life's power shines through us, even when we do not notice. We become a blessing to others then, simply by being as we are.

—Rachel Naomi Remen

First, blessing is not a technique we perform but a presence we embody. It's not an act we do to someone or something but a relationship we form with them that enables us all to be embraced in the presence of the unobstructed world.

—David Spangler

Our experience of grace as a blessing that comes into our lives unearned, without merit, calls forth the response of gratitude.
   —Margaret A. Burkhardt and Mary Gail Nagai-Jacobson

The Lord bless you and keep you; the Lord make his face shine upon you, and be gracious to you; the Lord lift up his countenance upon you and give you peace.
   —Numbers 6:24–26

For this I bless you most:
You give much and know not that you give at all.
   —Kahlil Gibran

Sharing   60 minutes

Closing Activity

Closing Words

May the blessing of light be on you—light without and light within. May the blessed sunlight shine on you and warm your heart till it glows like a great peat fire.
   —Old Celtic Blessing

Song

Announcements

Extinguishing the Candle

East: Brother Fire, thank you for warming our hearts.

South: Father Air, we thank you for inspiring us here.

West: Sister Water, thank you for the courage to be present to the flow of life.

North: Mother Earth, we thank you for grounding us here.

Leader: Spirit within, we take you with us to cherish until we meet again.

Leader's Guide

We hope that being a Soul to Soul group leader will be easy and enjoyable. You will take care of logistics and maintain the process which ensures a safe place to share deeply. Your group will appreciate your leadership!

Whether you recruit your group or are given a list of members by your congregation, it's a good idea to give each person a call or send them an email before the group starts. Introduce yourself, answer questions, and make sure each person has a copy of *Soul to Soul* and knows to read the Introduction and first gathering (Thick Stories) before the group first meets.

Soul to Soul groups focus on appreciative silent listening with no questions, advice, or judgment. Since this is a new way of listening for most, as leader, you'll guide your group as they learn the power of Soul to Soul listening. At the first meeting, the group will discuss and, if necessary, modify a covenant that each person agrees to abide by during the life of the group.

Most groups feel a little uncomfortable with the lack of response after someone's sharing. Assure the group that, in time, listening from the heart rather than from the mind can provide deep and meaningful benefits, while responding to someone who is sharing deeply is actually quite tricky. As time goes along and the silence becomes more intimate, your group will learn to appreciate the freedom that not responding gives to both the person sharing and those listening, and will recognize the healing and sacred nature of this silence. If there are any questions, contact us at our website, www.HearttoHeartBook.com.

Your Participation in the Group

As leader, you are both a facilitator and a participant. You will go first in sharing in the early gatherings to set the tone and show the way. We encourage you to go as deeply into the topic as you are willing. Your courage will pave the way for group members to also risk sharing at a deeper level. Remind the group that wisdom comes from speaking our truth and being heard. You'll maintain safety in the group by watching out for cross-talk, advice, and "fixing." You will also take on the role of timekeeper, to make sure everyone gets equal time to share. We have included suggested approximate times for each segment of the gathering to keep your group on track. Some leaders use a watch or a timer and signal the speaker with a small wave when their sharing time is coming to an end.

Once your group becomes accustomed to the gathering format, you may want to take turns leading. Sharing the leader's role can help the group mature, since everyone has an equal stake in the group. Even if the group rotates leadership at each session, you as overall leader should still oversee the entire program and attend to any problems that may come up.

Challenging Members

If someone forgets the "no cross-talk" agreement, you can refer to the covenant developed in the first gathering. There may be a group member who is consistently unable to fit into the structured process of sharing without comment or judgment. As leader, you may want to talk with this person after the group to make sure they are in agreement with the covenant. Sometimes people sign up for a group like this assuming that it is a discussion group. You may need to be firm in explaining that this is a sharing group, not a discussion group, and suggest that if they don't want to be part of a sharing group, they should probably not continue.

Preparation for the Gatherings

Leader's Notes for Each Gathering begin on page 141. Sometimes preparation is needed before a gathering, such as bringing tea lights for a ritual. Have your pre-gathering work done before people begin to arrive so you can be fully present to them when they get there.

Format for the Gatherings

Each gathering has the same format with the following elements:

Candle Lighting. One of the goals of Soul to Soul groups is to create a safe space for deep sharing. We do this by agreeing to act in ways that help create this safety by authorizing a leader to help us stay safe, and by using a format which informs participants exactly what is expected of them and allows them to prepare. A final way we create a sense of safe space is with a brief ritual. Rituals act out a hoped-for reality as a way of living into that hoped-for reality.

The candle-lighting ritual reminds us in a vivid way that we desire a safe space for sharing. It calls on the four directions to remind us of the powers beyond and within that will contribute to successful sharing within the safety of our circle. Lighting the candle gives us a continuing reminder during the gathering of the safe circle we've created. A closing ritual thanks those powers and opens up the circle.

At the starting time, ask your group to stand around the candle, placed on a center table with roughly equal numbers of people at the north, east, south, and west points (or as close as is practical). To begin, everyone turns to face east, and the people on that side of the candle read the east lines. Then all face south, and those folks read the south lines. Then west, then north in the same way:

East: Brother Fire, we invoke warmth. May our hearts be open to each other.

South: Father Air, we invoke inspiration. May our words be wise and kind.

West: Sister Water, we invoke the flow of life. May we have courage.

North: Mother Earth, we invoke groundedness. May we all be here in spirit as well as in body.

Once the group is seated around the candle and all is quiet, the leader reads the following line, then lights the candle:

Leader: Spirit within, we invoke depth. May we remember all we value.

It will take at least three repetitions before a new ritual like this becomes meaningful. Ask your group's indulgence to try it and take it seriously for three gatherings before making modifications. The fourth gathering will include a discussion about this ritual and a chance for the group to shape it to make it work for them. In the meantime, your attitude as the leader will make a real difference. Remember that the purpose of this ritual is to help people center in this space and open themselves to the qualities that will make this a good group. Important things take preparation. The candle you light should be a nice one, sitting in a nice holder, perhaps with a cloth under it to set it off. After you've explained to your group what you are going to do, take another breath or two to give this ritual some psychic space. Then nod to the east to begin. See if you can influence the timing of the reading with your eye contact.

Keep your group silent as they turn toward the four directions. When they are seated again, take a couple of breaths before you say your sentence and light the candle. If you enjoy the light of the flame for a breath or two before drawing back into your seat, they will, too. As you look up at your group members, smile, and begin the gathering, you seal the ritual and make it feel significant. Spiritual leaders call this the work of "holding sacred space," and it may feel a little weird or pretentious at first. You do it in the service of the group, as their leader, and if you keep that service in your heart, the group will thank you for taking the risk.

On Our Hearts. This is a time for sharing major highs and lows in participants' lives, not a check-in where everyone recounts each event of the week. Ask participants if anyone has a special joy or sorrow in their heart right now that they want the group to know about. Also mention any absent members.

Silence. Each gathering includes three minutes of silence, with the exception of the Shadow, Play, and Prayer sessions, where there are guided meditations. For each gathering, you'll find quotes, mantras, or brief meditations designed to help participants settle into the quiet—these are located in the Leader's Notes for Each Gathering. To indicate the end of the silence, say, "May your silence be a blessing to us" or "Thank you."

Shared Readings. Go around the circle, with each person offering one of the provided readings.

Sharing. Sharing is done in three rounds. Prompts for each round are in the Leader's Notes for Each Gathering. In general, the first round asks participants to briefly share a response to a specific question or participate in a short activity. Go first to model for the group, then continue around the circle.

The second round is an opportunity for participants to share something they felt about this topic while doing the preparation— a way they grew, something that touched them, or a story they wish to share. Each person has about four minutes. Go first to model for the group, then ask participants to share in any order. End with a moment of silence.

If there is time for a third round, you can start by saying how much time there is left and remind the group that the purpose of this last round is to comment on what they've heard or any other thoughts they have on the subject. It may be that not everyone will speak during the third round.

During the sharing, one person speaks at a time. The one who is sharing has the job of speaking deeply from the heart about the topic. Listeners have the task of keeping an appreciative silence and an open heart to what is shared. If someone does not want to speak, he or she may pass.

Closing Activity. This varies from gathering to gathering and is detailed in the Leader's Notes. It may be a brief time to share a word or two about how the member is feeling or a simple ritual to bring the gathering to a conclusion.

Closing Words. These are provided for each gathering and may be read by the leader or a person appointed by the leader.

Song. After the closing words are read, lead the group in singing "Thank You for Your Loving Hands" (page xiii). You might want to practice singing it at the start of each gathering until it becomes familiar.

Announcements. There may be a few announcements. Always consult the Leader's Notes about the next gathering so you can describe any special items you want participants to bring next time. Also, think about seasonal considerations. At the mid-November gathering, for instance, you may want to ask whether the group would prefer a holiday social gathering, a regular gathering, or no gathering toward the end of December.

Extinguishing the Candle. At the end of the gathering, take a moment to let people remember which direction they were. Ask them to stand in their original places and face east. Say, "Let's take a breath together, and then east can start." East is followed by south, west, and north:

East: Brother Fire, thank you for warming our hearts.

South:	Father Air, we thank you for inspiring us here.
West:	Sister Water, thank you for the courage to be present to the flow of life.
North:	Mother Earth, we thank you for grounding us here.

The people take their seats, and the leader reads the last line and extinguishes the candle.

| Leader: | Spirit within, we take you with us to cherish until we meet again. |

Once again, linger a breath and let the smoke waft into the room before you straighten up, make eye contact with your group, and return to ordinary time.

The Rewards

All these instructions may seem intimidating at first, but you'll find that after a few gatherings, it will all come very easily. You'll have the joy of watching your group grow together in spiritual exploration and create deep bonds of friendship. By the end of the fourteen gatherings, listening from the heart with no advice, judgment, and questions, which seemed mildly awkward at the beginning, will evolve into a warm, supportive, and sacred action. The group will learn that nothing needs to be said—our open-hearted presence is the best gift.

Leader's Notes for Each Gathering

These notes explain how to prepare for each gathering and describe how to facilitate the various segments of the gathering. Other special instructions are also included here.

THICK STORIES

Before the Gathering

Practice the song "Thank You for Your Loving Hands" if necessary (page xiii). Read the description of the first round of sharing (see Sharing, below) and think about your response so that you will be prepared to go first. Prepare a list of members' names, phone numbers, and email addresses. Place one copy of the list in the room where you will meet, along with name tags and pens.

At the Gathering

As people come in, ask them to check the list and make sure that their names, phone numbers, and email addresses are correct. Invite them to put on name tags.

Welcome and Explanations. When everyone has settled in, tell group members how glad you are that they are in the group and how much you're looking forward to getting to know them. Tell them that each gathering will last about an hour and a half to two hours. See if any group members need to be very strict about time (for public transportation or child care, for instance). Point out where the bathroom is. Ask members whether they are comfortable sharing their contact information with one another, and tell them that if they are, copies of the list will be provided next time.

Explain that each gathering will follow the same routine. The gatherings open with a candle lighting and On Our Hearts, which is a time for briefly sharing major highs and lows. This week, you'll be skipping On Our Hearts because of the extra components of this first meeting. Next come Silence and Shared Readings. The core of the gathering is the Sharing. Describe the three rounds of sharing (described on page 138). Explain that there is no cross-talk in rounds of sharing, but that participants are to listen deeply, from the heart. The sharing is followed by a closing activity, which is a brief ritual or exercise related to the topic. The gathering concludes with closing words, a song, announcements, and extinguishing the candle.

After reviewing the structure of the gatherings, say that you'll start the gathering now with the candle lighting.

Candle Lighting. Explain the candle lighting ritual (described on page 136) and carry it out.

Covenant. Go around the circle and let each person read a line of the covenant. After each line, ask the group questions like, Is everyone comfortable with this promise? Is there anyone who is uncomfortable with this? Can we all agree to this?
Adjust the covenant to fit your needs as you go along.

Silence. Explain that there will be three minutes of silence at each gathering, unless there is a guided meditation instead. Introduce the time of silence with this quotation:

Amid all the noise in our lives,
   we take this moment to sit in silence—
      to give thanks for another day;

to give thanks for all those in our lives
      who have brought us warmth and love;
to give thanks for the gift of life.
      —Tim Haley

Shared Readings. Ask a group member to read the first reading. Continue around the circle.

Sharing. For the first round of sharing (15 minutes), let each person briefly tell one thing that drew him or her to this group. Go first to model. For the second round of sharing, show the item you have brought that symbolizes for you the deep and meaningful parts of your life. The more deeply you share, the more deeply your group will share. After you have shared, ask others to share as they are ready (35 minutes). If a group member has forgotten to bring an item, ask this person to describe what they might have brought. In the third round, give group members the opportunity to share additional thoughts or to reflect on what others have shared (10 minutes). Because this first gathering has lots of additional elements, you may not have time for the third round.

Closing Activity. Invite the group to hold hands around the circle and have each member share a hope they have for their participation in the group and one or two words about how they are feeling. Be prepared to go first, and proceed around the circle.

COMPASSION

Before the Gathering

If the group has agreed to share contact information, make enough copies for everyone. Prepare for the Closing Activity by reading over the meditation several times.

At the Gathering

Silence. Introduce the time of silence with this reading:

The one journey that ultimately matters is the journey into the place of stillness deep within one's self. To reach that place is to be home; to fail to reach it is to be forever restless.
—Gordon Cosby

Sharing. For the first round, ask group members to share briefly an experience they've had in the past few weeks in giving, receiving, or observing compassion. Be prepared to go first, then proceed around the circle (15 minutes). In the second round, group members, speaking in any order, can share more deeply about compassion in their lives or share their experience with the activities and questions from their preparation (40 minutes). As time allows in the third round, those who wish to may share additional thoughts or reflect on what others have shared (10 minutes).

Closing Activity. Read the following meditation. The symbol "....." indicates that you should pause for the length of four to five normal breaths.

Jack Kornfield tells us that "the human heart has the extraordinary capacity to hold and transform the sorrows of life into a great stream of compassion." To begin this meditation on compassion, sit comfortably with your eyes closed or gaze in a relaxed manner at the candle burning in the center of the circle. Relax your body and breathe several times.....

Visualize your heart as it transforms the sorrows of your life into a stream of compassion. Imagine a light coming in through the top of your head, filling your whole body..... The light moves out of your heart and swirls around your body creating a gentle cloud or blanket of compassion. Rest in this peaceful time of self-compassion.....

144

Now think of someone close to you, someone you love. Become aware of their sorrows and hold that person in your heart. Again, imagine a light coming in through the top of your head and through your body..... Visualize the light flowing out through your heart toward this person you love, wrapping them in a gentle cloud or blanket of compassion.....

Now picture someone with whom you have difficulty. Open your compassionate heart to them. Picture them, wish them well and send them your compassionate light.....

After some time, breathe in a natural and restful way. Open your eyes slowly and peacefully.

BOUNDARIES

At the Gathering

Silence. Introduce the time of silence by saying:

As you focus on your breath, pay attention to its sensation as it moves in and out of your body, then count each breath in and each breath out in this way:
Breathe in "one." Breathe out "one."
Breathe in "two." Breathe out "two." Continue counting in silence.

Sharing. For the first round (15 minutes), ask group members to share their thoughts about a time they let down their boundaries in order to please others, or the ways boundaries have changed in their families. Go first to model sharing, then continue around the circle. For the second round, speaking in any order, members can share their feelings, stories, and experiences of boundaries or their experience with one of the activities from their preparation (35 minutes). As time allows, in the third round, those who wish to may share additional thoughts or reflect on what others have shared (10 minutes).

Closing Activity. Invite group members to hold hands around the circle and briefly share an insight or feeling about this gathering. Be prepared to go first, and continue around the circle.

TRUST

Before the Gathering

Read over the Closing Activity. At the end of the gathering, there will be time to discuss the candle-lighting ritual and a chance for the group to modify it, if necessary, to better fit the group. In order to refresh your understanding of the intent of the ritual, re-read the section explaining the candle lighting in the Leader's Guide (page 136).

At the Gathering

Silence. Introduce the silence with this reading:

> The soul wants silence—and when we give people excuses and permission to be silent in a circle of trust, the soul rises to the occasion, often with transforming results.
>
> Why does the soul love silence? The deepest answer I know invokes the mystery of where we came from and where we are headed. At birth, we emerged from the Great Silence into a world that constrains the soul; at death, we return to the Great Silence where the soul is once again free.
> —Parker J. Palmer

Sharing. For the first round, invite group members to describe briefly one of their trust teachers, whether kind or cruel. Be prepared to share first, then go around the circle (15 minutes). In the second round, speaking in any order, group members can share more deeply their feelings about trust or their experience with one of the activities from their preparation (35 minutes). Because of the discussion about the candle lighting, we suggest skipping the third round.

Closing Activity. Move the group to an open space so they can stand in a circle close to one another, shoulder to shoulder. One at a time, as members are willing, have one person stand in the center of the circle with arms crossed over the chest, knees locked. Go first to demonstrate. Tell the group you will lean slowly in any direction until you lose your balance. At that point the group will gently move you back to the center toward another point in the circle. Continue "falling" and being gently redirected for a few times. Give each person a turn to be the faller. Be sensitive to different physical abilities. A very fragile person might ask not to fall into the group, but to lean.

Return to the circle and be seated. Ask each person to say one word to describe the activity.

Discussion of the Candle-Lighting Ritual. Going around the circle, ask group members to share briefly their response to the candle-lighting ritual. Go last to keep from influencing opinions. See if there is a consensus on desired modifications. Move toward a trial change, if called for. Try this for several weeks, then have another discussion.

SPIRITUAL EXPERIENCES

At the Gathering

Candle Lighting. If there have been modifications to the candle-lighting ritual, go over them with the group before beginning.

Silence. Introduce the silence by saying:

> In your mind, go to a safe place, a place where you have known peace. This might be the woods, a sunny beach, a quiet spot in your church, or a flowering garden. Imagine yourself there quietly resting.

Sharing. In the first round, ask members to share a symbol they have chosen to remind them of a spiritual experience (15 minutes). If someone forgot to bring a symbol, ask them to share what they might have brought. For the second round, invite members, in any order, to share some of their most powerful spiritual experiences and share more deeply their thoughts about spiritual experience from the essay, readings, or activities (35 minutes). As time allows in the third round, those who wish to may share additional thoughts or reflect on what others have shared (10 minutes).

Closing Activity. Invite group members to hold hands around the circle and each say one or two words about how they are feeling or share an insight they have had at this gathering. Be prepared to go first, and proceed around the circle.

ADDICTION

Before the Gathering

Watch for the likelihood that people will begin to share not their own addictions but their pain over the addictions of others. Acknowledge their pain, but ask them to focus on their own addictions. You may also get some resistance from people who find the word "addiction" so negative that they are unwilling to apply it to themselves. There's no need to fight this. Just say, "Okay, bad habits," and let them continue to share.

At the Gathering

Silence. Introduce the silence by saying:

> Go around the circle in your mind, remembering remarks made during On Our Hearts. Send loving feelings to each person in the group, remembering those who are missing. Some send love to others by visualizing sending light out through one's heart to others.

Sharing. For the first round, ask group members to share whatever they are willing to from their list of addictive behaviors. Go first to model for the group, and then go around the circle (15 minutes). In the second round, invite group members, in any order, to share more deeply about either a situation they face with an addictive behavior, or stories and feelings they have about this topic (35 minutes). As time allows, those who wish to may share additional thoughts or reflect on what others have shared (10 minutes).

Closing Activity. Invite the group to hold hands around the circle and each share an insight they have had or say one or two words about how they are feeling. Be prepared to go first, and proceed around the circle.

CALLING

Before the Gathering

Cut index cards into thirds or quarters. You should have approximately ten pieces for each person. Put the pieces in a small basket or bowl. Bring pencils or pens.

At the Gathering

Silence. Introduce the silence by saying:

149

We will say a mantra on the in-breath and the out-breath. You might say to yourself: "Breathe in love, breathe out peace" or "Spirit in, spirit out."

Do this over and over, becoming more relaxed with every breath.

Sharing. For the first round (15 minutes), ask group members to share briefly the qualities and descriptions of their true selves, as discovered in Activity 1. If someone didn't do this activity, ask them to share what action or task comes easily to them, what is effortless. For the second round, invite members, in any order, to share about their experiences of calling, or memories and feelings related to calling that arose from the essay, readings, or activities (35 minutes). As time allows in the third round, members may share additional thoughts or reflect on what others have shared (10 minutes).

Closing Activity. Put the basket of papers in the center of the table, next to the candle. Pass out pencils and pens as needed. Tell the group, "We are going to share the gifts of the spirit and the deep gladness we see in each other."

Focus on one person at a time, starting with the person to your right. Ask everyone to write on a card in one or two words a gift or positive attribute of that person, such as: cheerful, intuitive, organized, generous, or great listener. Have the group read their words out loud and pass the cards to the person described. Go around the group, ending with yourself.

SHADOW

Before the Gathering

Read over the Closing Activity.

At the Gathering

Guided Meditation. Lead the guided meditation with the following words. The symbol "....." indicates that you should pause for the length of four to five normal breaths.

> We will do a relaxation meditation during our time of silence.
> Breath normally.....
> Focus on your neck and face and let them relax. Let them
> relax.....
> After a few breaths, focus on your back and arms. Let them
> relax.....
> Focus on your stomach and hips. Let them relax.....
> Then your legs and feet.....
> Continue to breathe in and out in a very relaxed way.

Sharing. For the first round (15 minutes), ask participants to share one shadow aspect and show the shadow costume they brought. Go first, then continue around the circle. If someone didn't bring anything, ask them to describe the costume they might have brought. For the second round, speaking in any order, group members can share more deeply their feelings and stories about the shadow. They may talk about one of the activities or a part of the essay or quotations that touched their heart (35 minutes). As time allows in the third round, members may share additional thoughts or reflect on what others have shared (10 minutes).

Closing Activity. Have everyone put on or make use of the shadow symbol they brought and enjoy a few chaotic minutes of interacting playfully with each other's shadow and shadow objects. Have fun!

AFTER DEATH

At the Gathering

Silence. Introduce the silence with this reading:

In quietness and in trust shall be your strength.
—Isaiah 30:15

Sharing. For the first round (15 minutes), ask group members to briefly describe an experience that was formative for them in creating their current belief about what happens after death. Go first to model sharing, then continue around the circle. For the second round, speaking in any order, participants may share their views on life after death by reading their poems or essays, showing their pictures, or briefly telling the group about their beliefs (35 minutes). As time allows for the third round, those who wish to may share additional thoughts or reflect on what others have shared (10 minutes).

Closing Activity. Invite group members to hold hands around the circle and briefly share an insight or feeling about this gathering. Be prepared to go first, and continue around the circle.

PLAY

At the Gathering

Guided Meditation. Lead the guided meditation with the following words. The symbol "....." indicates that you should pause for the length of four to five normal breaths.

We will do this meditation during our time of silence.
You can play with the silence like a baby plays with its blanket. Take a deep breath, relax, and let it cover you. You

are safe here, you can rest here. You don't have to do anything or accomplish anything or tend to anybody just now. Just be.....

You can play with your breathing the way a toddler plays with a new toy. Turn it over and over intently. Notice everything—how it goes in and out. How it feels in your nostrils, your throat, your belly. What it sounds like, what it is like. Just play.....

You can listen to the silence the way a teenager listens to a new hit. Listen for every nuance, every cough, every hum of light and swish of passing car. Just listen.....

You can ponder whatever thought comes to you the way a young adult ponders a new love, with tenderness and wonder and excitement. Just ponder.....

    —Christine Robinson

Sharing. For the first round, go around the circle and let people share briefly a childhood activity that brings back memories of play (15 minutes). In the second round, group members, speaking in any order, can share more deeply about the play in their lives or share their experience with the activities and questions from their preparation (35 minutes). As time allows in the third round, members may share additional thoughts or reflect on what others have shared (10 minutes).

Closing Activity. Group members were asked to think about how to incorporate more play into their lives and to bring an item symbolizing that resolve. Give everyone a chance to put their item on the table and say a few words about their hopes and plans. When all items are on the table, call attention to the collage of good intentions and invite everyone to cheer "Hip hip hooray!" three times.

PRAYER

Before the Gathering

Bring a tea light or other candle for each member of your group for the closing activity. Put them on the center table before the gathering starts.

At the Gathering

Metta or Loving Kindness Meditation. Tell your group about the meditation by saying the following:

Instead of a time of silence, today we're going to do a guided prayer or meditation which comes from the Buddhist tradition. It is called "metta," or loving kindness meditation. I'll guide you through the four parts, each of which will focus our loving kindness on a different person. The first person you will focus on is yourself. For the second part, choose a loved one to focus on. For the third, choose someone you encounter often but hardly know—your child's teacher, perhaps, or a person who works down the hall from you. The fourth person you'll focus on is someone you have anger or issues with. I'll guide you through this, but before we start you need to have in mind your four people: yourself, a loved one, someone you don't know well, and someone you have issues with.

Are you ready?

Settle yourself comfortably, and take a few deep breaths. The first subject of our meditation is ourselves, so open your heart to yourself. Picture yourself in your mind's eye as you listen to these words and repeat them to yourself:

[Speak slowly.]

154

May I be filled with loving kindness
May I be well
May I be peaceful and at ease
May I be whole.

[Slowly repeat the above four sentences.]
[Leave a little silence.] Now, focus your attention on the loved one you chose, picturing them in your mind's eye. [Give them a short time to do this, and continue.]

May you be filled with loving kindness
May you be well
May you be peaceful and at ease
May you be whole.

[Repeat and leave some silence before going on.]
Now change your focus to the person you chose who you encounter but don't know well. Think of their name, picture their face. [Give them a moment to do this, then continue in the same way.]

Now, change your focus again, to the person with whom you have issues. Try to keep that open heart, and picture their face in your mind's eye. [Give them a moment to do this, and then say the words of the prayer through twice more.]

Now, I invite you to focus on yourself once again. Say to yourself,

May I be filled with loving kindness
May I be well
May I be peaceful and at ease
May I be whole.

Sharing. For the first round, ask group members to briefly share a reaction to the Loving Kindness Meditation (15 minutes). In the second round, group members, speaking in any order, can share about prayer in their lives or share their experience with the activitics and questions from their preparation (35 minutes). As time allows in the third round, members may share additional thoughts or reflect on what others have shared (10 minutes).

Closing Activity. Each person will have an opportunity to light a prayer candle to close this session. Give people a moment to think about what or who they want to light their candle for. After they light the candle, they may say what it is for, if they wish. Go first to model.

RESILIENCE

Before the Gathering

Prepare by reading over the meditation in the Closing Activity several times.

At the Gathering

Silence. Introduce the silence with this reading:

> May our shared silence be a blessing on our hearts, on this community, and may this blessing extend outward to grace the wider world.
> —Maureen Killoran

Sharing. For the first round, ask group members to share their experience with the bird/boat exercise (15 minutes). For the second round, invite members, in any order, to share more deeply about resilience, or give their reactions to the essay, readings, or activities (35 minutes). As time allows in the third round, those who wish to may share additional thoughts or reflect on what others have shared (10 minutes).

Closing Activity. Ask the group to close their eyes and settle into silence and restfulness with a few breaths. Read the following meditation slowly. The symbol "....." indicates that you should pause for the length of four to five normal breaths.

> Close your eyes.....
> Breathe deeply, slowly, and gently.....
> Imagine your body is the deep, calm ocean.....
> Your head and thoughts are ripples and waves on the surface.....
> Now imagine the ripples and waves are higher up, way above your head.
> Your body is grounded in stillness; let the waves do what they like.....
> The ripples on the surface might be thoughts or outer events.
> They are minute compared to your body, the ocean, you, the solid strength within.
> Like an iceberg where a greater percentage is below the surface.....
> Now imagine your feet are rooted deep within the earth, creating a strong and sturdy structure.....
> Even if waves were to come, they would simply wash over you with little effect.....
> Outer events are not you.
> Your thoughts are not you.
> Other people's interpretations of you are not you.
> The ripples and waves are only temporary.....
> Deep within you is a place of quiet, peace, and calm.
> Somewhere you can go wherever you are.
> You can lessen the burden of surface waves by keeping in touch with the calm seas within.....
> Ripples come; ripples go.
> —Paul Foreman

AGING

At the Gathering

Silence. Introduce the silence with the following words:

Listen to this verse:
Be still, and know that I am God!
  —Psalm 46:10

Close your eyes. As I repeat the verse, I will leave off a word or
  two each time.
Be still and know that I am God.
Be still and know that I am
Be still and know
Be still
Be
You may want to repeat that to yourself several times in the
  silence.

Sharing. Watch for the possibility that group members may begin
to share not their own aging, but that of others, perhaps older parents. Begin the sharing time by reading the following passage from
this gathering's essay to encourage members to look at their own
aging, regardless of how old they are.

We begin graceful aging quite young, actually—or we begin
a life-long habit of denial. When we first realize that we just
can't eat as much as we used to without gaining weight, when
we start hearing the ticking of our reproductive clock, . . . all
these are warm-ups for the rigors of aging.

For the first round, ask group members to share briefly an age-
related loss they have experienced in the last few years. Be prepared
to go first, then proceed around the circle (15 minutes). In the second round, group members, speaking in any order, can share more

deeply about aging in their lives or share their experience with the activities and questions from their preparation (35 minutes). As time allows in the third round, members may share additional thoughts or reflect on what others have shared (10 minutes).

Closing Activity. Invite group members to hold hands around the circle and each say one or two words about how they are feeling or share an insight they have had at this gathering. Be prepared to go first, and proceed around the circle.

BLESSINGS

Before the Gathering

Read over the Closing Activity. Make an index card for each person in the group with the following written on it: "We bless you as this group ends and wish _____ for you as you go forth." Fill in the blank on each person's card with your wish for that person, such as health, happiness, peace, or strength. Be sure to make a card for yourself. Put the cards face down on the table. At the closing activity, lay the cards out face up around the candle on the table.

At the Gathering

Silence. Introduce the silence with this reading:

Here, in this space, we are called to weave the web of human community. May we pause, and in our silence, may we lift up at least one blessing, one joy, no matter how small, that has touched our life this week.
—Maureen Killoran

Sharing. For the first round (15 minutes), ask participants to name one blessing in their life. Go first to model. Go around the circle several times, with each person naming one blessing. If a person runs out of ideas, they can pass. Continue until most people have run out of blessings. In the second round, speaking in any order, group members can share more deeply their feelings and stories about blessings. They may talk about one of the activities or a part of the essay or quotations that touched their heart (35 minutes). As time allows in the third round, members may share additional thoughts or reflect on what others have shared (10 minutes).

Closing Activity. Put the index cards face up around the candle and put a chair in the center of the circle next to the table. Introduce the closing activity by saying:

> Remember when we came together at our first gathering and shared our Thick Stories? Since that time we've heard so many stories. We've shared our lives and our souls. We've listened with open hearts and embraced each other's lives. Today we'll do a ritual to celebrate our appreciation for one another, our closeness, this final meeting, and the life we've lived together. We're going to bless each other by doing something called the "laying on of hands," which is simply touching the person to be blessed.

Ask someone to go first; have him or her sit in the chair.

Ask someone to go second; he or she will take the first person's card. Put a hand on the first person's shoulder, arms, or head and invite the rest of the group (including the reader) to do the same.

Pause for a few breaths of silence. Nod at the reader to read the card. Let there be another breath or two of silence after the reading.

Then pick up your hands and indicate that the others should do so also.

The first person stands, the second sits, and a volunteer picks the card of the second person. Repeat.

You go last, and the first person to be blessed will read your card.

(This blessing is structured so that the person who has just been blessed doesn't have to immediately read. People sometimes get a bit choked up over this powerful ritual.)